TIMELESS
WISDOMS

VOLUME ONE

To Mike + Alisha Heyer

L.L.

Dr. John-Roger

TIMELESS WISDOMS

VOLUME ONE

John-Roger, D.S.S.

Mandeville Press
Los Angeles, California

Mandeville Press
P.O. Box 513935
Los Angeles, California 90051-1935
323-737-4055
jrbooks@mandevillepress.org
www.mandevillepress.org

Printed in the United States of America
ISBN 10: 1-893020-47-9
ISBN 13: 978-1-893020-47-4
LCCN: 2007941092

Acknowledgments

My thanks to Nat Sharratt for running by me everything involved with *Timeless Wisdoms* so that I could do it. Thanks, also, to these people, who assisted with the book: Betsy Alexander, compiler and editor; David Sand, design; Virginia Rose and Bambi Scott, proofing; Lisa Liddy, graphics; Barbara Wieland, for providing some information from the John-Roger Library and Archives; and Vincent Dupont, Mandeville Press.

Other Books by John-Roger

Blessings of Light
The Consciousness of Soul
Divine Essence
Dream Voyages
Forgiveness – The Key to the Kingdom
Fulfilling Your Spiritual Promise
God Is Your Partner
Inner Worlds of Meditation
Journey of a Soul
Living Love from the Spiritual Heart
Loving Each Day
Loving Each Day for Moms & Dads
Loving Each Day for Peacemakers
Manual on Using the Light
Momentum: Letting Love Lead (with Paul Kaye)
Passage Into Spirit
The Path to Mastership
The Power Within You
Psychic Protection
Relationships: Love, Marriage and Spirit
The Rest of Your Life (with Paul Kaye)
Sex, Spirit and You
The Spiritual Family
Spiritual High (with Michael McBay, M.D.)
The Spiritual Promise
Spiritual Warrior: The Art of Spiritual Living
The Tao of Spirit
Walking with the Lord
The Way Out Book
Wealth & Higher Consciousness
What's It Like Being You? (with Paul Kaye)
When Are You Coming Home? (with Pauli Sanderson)

Contents

Contents

Preface

Dr. John-Roger has been speaking for almost forty-five years about the spiritual realities he has discovered. A naturally curious and questioning person, he has explored with an open mind, clear eyes, and a courageous heart the vast inner and outer universes of Spirit. He has a unique ability to articulate truths about this physical-level life as well as the ineffable experiences of Spirit, and encouraged by his loving guidance, those of us studying with him have also explored the paths he has shone the light on. He has always said that what he has learned, we can learn—not just mentally, through amassing words and concepts, but through our own direct experience.

John-Roger has often told us that he is not saying anything new but is putting into words for our time the timeless wisdoms of lovers and knowers of God through the ages. And, riding on the pure energy of Spirit that he carries with him, what words they are—clear, pithy, humorous, profound, encouraging, and always loving and supportive of our greater awareness.

Our hearts have been lifted with the assurance that not one Soul will be lost.

We've increased our compassion as we have understood that everyone is doing the best they can with what they know.

We've been less embarrassed when we've heard that anything we have done, he, in all his existences, has also done.

We've become more willing to smile and laugh at our challenges because he has told us—and demonstrated—that if it will be funny later, it's funny now.

We've learned to be more honest with ourselves and others, prodded by the realization that no matter how thin you slice it, it's still baloney.

We've been lovingly embraced in times of grief when we have known the inner reality of his promise, "I am always with you."

And we are expanding more into the most profound truth that he and other mystics and teachers have experienced: you are divine.

Here, then, are some of the timeless wisdoms of John-Roger.

Betsy Alexander

Out of God Come All Things

There is only one message from God, although there are many ways that it's said and many ways that it's expressed. That one message is that all things come from God. Everything has its existence because God is.

There is great security in knowing this. God is multidimensional; God is everywhere, in all things and in all levels of consciousness. So the things that appear to be negative are only learning devices, not punishments. And Jesus said that "when you have done it to the least one of these, you have done it to me" (Matthew 25:40). Because all things come out of God, if we become prejudiced against one, we have become prejudiced against the awakening of our own consciousness of love.

1

God Loves All of Its Creation

In the Bible, it says that God created the world and human beings, and He saw that it was very good. That means that God loves it and loves us. God is maintaining us here and has also given us the ability to build and change according to our own will.

You are loved just as you are right now. Get that really clear in your heart. There is nothing you have to do differently to be loved by God. Who you are is enough in itself. This is the positive inner reality, and it's the truth about you. If the way you are and the way you behave aren't joy-producing for you, then you have the right and the ability to change. Regardless, God's love is consistently available to you.

There is so much there for you, once you open yourself to it and begin to work consciously on levels higher than that of Earth. It's all a manifestation of love. Love is the matrix that makes it all possible. The energy of Spirit is the essence, and this is the age of living love. This living love manifests each time you enter into the love of the spiritual heart. The message of this age is just that God's love is manifest here and now, within each person. When love is manifested and precipitated down, accepted and expressed, there is no more to be done.

Not One Soul Will Be Lost

Everyone will get off the cycle of return eventually. Everyone will make it. And if you stay within the teachings and the consciousness of the Mystical Traveler, you can be free of the cycle of return this lifetime. So don't worry about it; don't be concerned. Spirit is not worried. Your Soul is not worried. It knows the perfection. It sees it already accomplished. All you have to do is walk the body and the consciousness through the steps of the process.

There is rejoicing in Spirit when you come home. The way is prepared, and the door is open. All you need do is walk in and claim your heritage.

You Are Divine

A lot of people say, "There has to be something better than this. There has to be a lot more than this." There *is* a lot more than this, but not necessarily on the physical level. Wherever you are, no matter what you are doing or what you have with you, you can have the greatest experience possible: the awareness that you are a child of God and are divine. The one you have been waiting for is already here—and has been here for a long time. You are the spiritual being you've been searching to find. At some time, within your inner consciousness, you vowed to become aware of your divinity. Eternally, that awareness is yours. You are the one you seek. You are the divine one, the promised one, the Beloved, and indeed you are the Light, you are divine, and you are in a state of becoming aware of what you already are.

You may shut down your awareness of God by putting your faith in the world, professing God's greatness out there. But God's greatness isn't out there. It's inside you. If you cannot find God within yourself, I will guarantee you, you cannot find God anywhere else. And when you start to find God in yourself, then you can find God anywhere. When you totally find God in yourself, then you *will* find that God is everywhere.

You are God's child, no matter what you are doing. You are never separated from God, no matter what you do. There is no expression that is not God's expression. Some expressions do not reflect the glory of God as completely as others. Which expressions you demonstrate is always up to you. If you think you are too unworthy for the Lord to visit you, you are experiencing the negative power. You are worthy of God because you are one with God. You have never been separate; it is only the illusion of this physical level that causes you to think so.

So don't be ashamed of what or who you are. You are divine. You are perfect. If the human condition doesn't always reflect the perfection, that's because there is no way to manifest the perfection here. You can't do it. The Traveler can't do it. Nobody can do it. So don't worry about it. To participate in Spirit, you don't have to flex your muscles or pull in your stomach, lose weight or gain weight, have hair or be bald, or anything else because those things have nothing to do with the divine energy of Spirit. Any negativity is just pointing out the next thing for you to work on and to bring across into the Divinity, until one day, and truthfully so, it will all be divine and you will know it as that. There will still be negativity, and there will still be positivity, and you will see it all equally as the Divine. That is your heritage.

All you have to do is awaken to that and then know it. And when in doubt, be loving. Let love be your guiding star. Let it be your guide, your breath, your life. Then you live in the heart of God and are renewed every moment through His love.

You Are a Soul

The Soul is love, joy, happiness, peace, thanksgiving, charity, benevolence. The Soul is all the positive qualities.

The Soul is your connection to God's loving heart. It is living water to quench your thirst, living food to nourish you, the living breath that gives you life.

The Soul's first name is Love, its middle name is Truth, and its last name is Everlasting. Love and Truth Everlasting.

The Soul (which is who you are) is a sacred, integral unit of energy, so beautiful that the whole cosmos and all the universes are contained within it. It is a prototype of all existence, complete in one energy unit. There is nothing that exists anywhere in the universes of which you are not a part, through the energy of the Soul. Thoughts cannot conceive the greatness of the Soul. You can't find the majesty of the Soul in science books or math books. You may not even be able to consciously look and find a key that awakens something inside of you a little more than

11

before. So all you can do is let go and say, "It's beyond my mental ability."

Still, when you are traveling through this life and attending to your daily routine, there are times when you feel the Light radiate to you, and you say, "Oh, my God, thank you for Your blessings." You feel momentarily blissed out. That's just an inkling of the Soul you are. And the Soul is everywhere. It's in the laughter. It's in the twinkle in the eyes. It's in the touch. It's in the empathy you experience when someone else is hurting. It's in the joy you experience when someone you love is happy. It's in all of that and more.

You do experience the Soul directly, not by reflection or interpretation, but directly. You get glimpses of what *is*. You get glimpses of knowing. Loving encompasses and fills everything. Joy shines inwardly. The trials of the world fade in power. All becomes one. You know your source and your comings and your goings from that source. All needs are already fulfilled, and there is nothing except loving communion with God. These are small signposts of Soul's experience.

Above all, the Soul is hopelessly and incorrigibly living love. It is the lover. It goes on in blissful ignorance of the pain and suffering experienced by the personality, emotions, mind, and imagination. The more loving you are, the more you free yourself to experience the Soul, and when you reach the Soul level, there is only a knowingness of God that does not rely on the body, mind, emotions, or imagination. It just is. In Soul awareness, there are no thoughts about God or feelings about God, and you are not imagining how God will be or should be. You are not involved in your image of God. You are simply aware of God.

Find Out Who You Really Are

First you learn who you are. And when you learn who the real self is, the false images fall away. The person you thought you were, the religion you thought you were, the philosophy you thought you were—these may fall away. You may find out that all of these philosophies that you've been adhering to just don't work, but you may be afraid to throw them away because you don't know what will take their place. When you get rid of the things that don't work, you will find the true self.

If you could just once see within the true self, if you could get that image just once in your consciousness for a fraction of a second, you could go on for the rest of your life using that as an inner guiding light. And to live from the level of your true self, you give yourself over to the truth of your own beingness completely. Then you find yourself moving into an awareness of your Soul consciousness, and in that you find your freedom. What it comes down to, always and forever, is the commitment to yourself, and that starts when, ten billion times a day, ten billion percent, you commit to the upliftment and the unfoldment that is your spiritual nature. You commit yourself to yourself—not to the personality or the emotions or the body or the wallet, but to that very essence of God that we identify as the Soul.

So enter into the warmth and graciousness of God within you. Go inside to Spirit, to God, to your own loving nature. Don't go inside and look at your emotions, or all you'll see is upset. Don't go inside and look at your mind; it will keep pushing you back out here, and you'll never see anything else. Go past those levels and you'll start moving into some of the most glorious territories that have yet to be investigated.

That very one you're looking for is in your heart, and the very one you've been after has always been here. If you really get that, it stirs deep inside you, beyond any place of comprehension, and goes to the place of understanding. That is the place where you say, "Yes, yes, yes, yes."

This divinity is yours for the taking. You weren't placed on the planet to be a beggar. These things are yours already, and all you need do is accept them. Your true self is perfect. You are divine. All things are given to you when you recognize who you are.

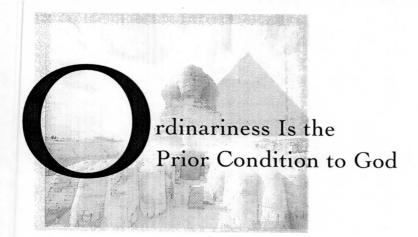Ordinariness Is the Prior Condition to God

We're all ordinary, which is the prior condition to God. When we see ourselves as special, we're actually moving further away from Spirit than when we're just ordinary.

This spiritual life is not necessarily conspicuous. Much more often, it is quiet and simple. And as you move more into the Spirit within you, someone looking from the outside might not notice the difference in you, which can be a real slap to the ego, so the ego may want to reassert itself, out of self-importance. But if you are in your ego, you are not in your Soul. You will know you are in your Soul when you are just being ordinary, just living your life simply and directly, doing what is in front of you without looking for recognition.

You Are a Multidimensional Being

You are on all levels of Light. Right now, in this moment, you are already in Soul consciousness, and you don't need to do anything except recognize it. Your opportunity is to become totally aware and completely capable of maintaining multidimensional awareness.

The reason you can have spiritual awareness on many levels is because the Soul manifests itself on many levels. On the physical plane, you have the realization of your Soul through the physical body; on the astral realm, through the imagination; on the causal, through the emotions; on the mental, through the mind; on the etheric, through a state of preparation; on the Soul realm, in a state of being; on the realm just above that, in a state of total awareness; and on the realm above that, in a state of pure Spirit or God consciousness. These, then, are eight possible states of Soul awareness. A wondrous God set up all this.

The multilevels of consciousness present inside you are

linked together in such a way that you can experience an awareness of them. To be consciously aware of any or all of these levels, you need only expand the consciousness to encompass them. The way to expand the consciousness instantly is to move directly into the Soul, which has all vision, all knowledge. It takes great discernment to do this, and when you do, you will experience the Soul consciously.

Prior to that, you are "dead" to this level when you are most alive to the Soul level. This is because in the spiritual realms of Soul, there is no time and no memory. It is spontaneous awareness. You do not bring back *memory* of that level to the physical level. What you can do is move back and forth between the levels quickly; you bridge the levels more and more swiftly, so that you develop multidimensional awareness by *having* it, not by remembering it. It is not a process of memory. It is actually a process of spontaneously moving between one level and the other, until you can do it so quickly that it appears you are aware of both levels simultaneously.

As you develop your ability to do this, you may find yourself moving in and out of Soul consciousness many times. The trick is to recognize when that shift happens and still maintain Soul consciousness. Until you can do that, it is okay to keep moving in and out of Soul consciousness. That will give you practice, and practicing joy and loving is more fun than practicing depression, anxiety, and fear. Put yourself in training for Soul consciousness by practicing the positive aspects of living and loving.

Also, give yourself permission to move through a range of expressions and experiences in this life, knowing they are all part of the human condition and part of your multidimensional beingness. You must be grounded here on the earth, as well as have awareness of Soul and Spirit. All must be balanced, and then you can move forward. When all is in balance, the Father's will and yours become one so that there is no struggle between "Thy will be done" and "my will be done." You ask that the Father's will be done, through you, by you, as you.

So be smart. Get into the Spirit and use that to flood through all the other levels. Be 100 percent everywhere in Spirit. It's the only way to experience multidimensional consciousness. Any other way is failure and illusion.

The Christ Resides in You

The Bible speaks of God's "only begotten Son" (John 3:16). That Son, that Christ Consciousness, is in each one of us, and it is the invisible part of us, the God part of us. When Jesus manifested that Christ Spirit in the world, it became easier for us to recognize it and realize that each of us possesses a part of that within ourselves. St. Paul wrote, "Let this mind be in you, which was also in Christ Jesus" (Philippians 2:5). This means that you are one with the Christ within and that God is totally present with you. Your challenge is to reach inside yourself and discover the God part and to work with it all the time. It is a never-ending process.

When you turn inside of yourself and consciously, purposefully, and directly reach for those things that enhance the Spirit within, you experience the strength of the Soul coming up inside of you. You experience a joy that has nothing to do with this level. You know an integrity within you that lifts you up and steady strength that sustains you through all things. That prepares a place for the Christ Consciousness to enter. You create a form into which the Beloved may come. People have waited for two thousand years for the King of Kings to appear in the sky and light up the world, but the King of Kings must first appear in *your* heart and light up *your* world. And that only happens when you have prepared that place inside of you where it can appear and live as your guiding Light.

So if you would live in the Soul and Spirit, you must be loyal to the Soul and the nature of the Soul, which is truthful, honest, and unconditionally loving. How do you do that? By dedicating yourself to the spiritual force within you, which is called the Christ, and making it the number one priority in your life.

The Traveler teaches about the sacrifice of what is negative and limited in your consciousness—but sacrifice so that you may expand into what is positive and uplifting, so that you may discover your own Christ Consciousness. When you won't sacrifice your anger for your loving expression, when you won't sacrifice your self-righteousness (which is "wrongeousness") for kindness and loving words, when you won't sacrifice your point of view for the highest good, then you are not living the Christ Consciousness. You are not living in grace.

But when you direct yourself towards the expression

of the Christ, you have the Christ Consciousness on your side. If you go against it, you have a lot of nothing on your side. So know that you are the only one who can delay or block your progress. You are the only one who can cloud your awareness. By the same token, you are the only one who can recognize the Christ within. You are the one who can make the Christ a living reality in your life and who can demonstrate the unconditional loving and forgiveness that indicate the presence of the Christ.

The awakening into the Christ may not be entirely pleasant. You have to let go of all the things you thought were necessary; otherwise, you do not inherit that which is the Christ. So when you pray, pray for the strength to overcome all negative aspects, the wisdom to guide you into all positive aspects, and the ability to stay focused on the Traveler as you are lifted into Soul consciousness, into the realization of your true self, into the recognition of the Christ.

You awaken to the Light and to the inner Christ through loving, laughter, empathy, and involvement with all life as it presents itself to you. As you move through all the experiences that come to you, both in the outer world and in the inner levels of your consciousness, and as you use empathy, loving, and forgiveness as the criteria for your behavior, you awaken to the inner wisdom of the Christ.

It is a JOYFUL day when you can know the Christ within. When you can live and demonstrate that beingness, it is an even greater day. And when you can look out and see the Christ in others, you are indeed blessed and beloved of God.

For the Highest Good of All Concerned

When we speak of the highest good, we speak of the highest God form, the God of all things. And when you honestly ask for things "for my highest good," your experiences *will* be for your highest good. If you find yourself being blocked in your pursuit of a particular goal, you might be wise to step back, take another look at your actions and motivations, and reevaluate whether the goal is for your highest good and the highest good of those around you.

And when you are an initiate of the Traveler and are working closely and consciously with Spirit, there is no need to ask for anything beyond whatever is for your highest good for your next level of unfoldment. All things are already being brought to you to lift you, to purify you, to prepare you to receive the keys of God's kingdom. And when you ask for the Light for the highest good in relation to something you want, it is then also important to let it go and forget about it. Just trust that if it's for the highest good, it will come forward, and if it isn't, it most likely won't.

Societies will fall many, many times in the evolution of the planet, and governments will come and go; that is the nature of this planet. But the Spirit stays forever. The key is this: reach always into the Spirit for the highest good of all and perceive all situations from that point.

Living In God's Holy Thoughts

The Light is the energy of Spirit that pervades all levels of consciousness. It is an energy that is of God. It is pure, uncorrupted, and available for our use.

The Light is in every aspect of your experience and your expression. You have never been less than the Light. That's who you are in the fullness and the glory of all your consciousness. And the Light is not sitting around, chanting and looking holy all day. The Light is the total beingness of all consciousness, on all levels, at all times. The Light is everywhere. When you accept that, you've made your first step.

"Light for the highest good" is a complete prayer. Nothing else is necessary. It will fulfill every need. No one really has control over the Light, but if you're attuned to the Light of Christ, you can ask that it be sent for the highest good to those people or situations that you feel could use it. If it can go for the highest good, it will go. And if it can't, it won't. By asking for the Light, you can be in a

29

state of constant prayer for the upliftment of everyone, full of love for the essence of that beingness. Then wherever you go, people will thank God that you're there. And that's really nice.

It also assists your Soul's growth when you silently send the Light to others. Those who know the Light and want to know and experience more are those who receive responsibilities for everyone with whom they come in contact. This is a load that may scare many people away, but the load is just this: when you go out into the world, always ask for the Light to surround and protect you and to move ahead of you for the highest good. And as you do this, remember that the spiritual heart is the center from which you work in your out-flowing of love. When people start coming too close to you, place the Light between you and them, and let the Light take the karma. The Light can handle it. All you have to do is maintain your awareness of the Light and place each situation and person you encounter into the Light.

There are a lot of ways to hold the Light and send the Light and work with the Light. One way is that as soon as someone tells you about a situation, just pass it right into the consciousness of the Light. Before that person even finishes getting the words out, it's gone. And treat everybody with kindness and consideration. Let people learn of your Light by demonstrating it in the way you live your life, rather than just by your words.

As an initiate of the Traveler progressing through the various levels of initiation, you become more and more powerful as you become more and more closely attuned to the Light and the Sound and the source within you that is God. Your very thoughts become prayers. And one of the most profound prayers you can whisper within the depth of your being is, "Father, Thy will be done." Then let go and let God work with you. When you utter that prayer in total sincerity and integrity, you bring yourself into alignment with Spirit and the plan God has for you in this life and for all eternity.

MSIA Teaches the Awakening in Love

The Movement of Spiritual Inner Awareness is an esoteric mystery school, meaning that it is an inner process of moving into Soul Transcendence. MSIA is here to present points of view to you and to present ways that can work for you. MSIA didn't come forward to start anything new, for there is no need for it. The truth is on the planet and has always been here. There has been no dark age when truth was removed from the planet. People just went into darkness in their minds and consciousnesses and changed what was here to suit themselves.

MSIA's outward expression is to bring people into a balance of working with each other and to bring greater conscious knowledge and understanding to each person. Other groups may teach awakening through anguish, pain, self-denial, abnegation, or fear. We don't teach that. There would be little joy in that path, and the presence of joy is one of the best indicators that the Spirit is present—joy and love.

This love we teach in MSIA is the love of understanding, acceptance, and support. It's the love that says, "Whatever you do is fine. I'll assist you, and I'll lift you." It's a peaceful, easy-going, flowing love. Everyone in your life can help you get in touch with the many aspects of yourself that are within you, and everyone can assist you in awakening to your loving. As you continually involve yourself in your own movement of spiritual inner awareness, your awakening will happen in its own natural rhythm. As you awaken, you can anchor Spirit in your life here, and, through attunement, you can discover Spirit and bring It to this level.

MSIA teaches you to tune in to what is already inside you, what is already there. MSIA works to show you how to do for yourself what you already know how to do but have forgotten. It isn't so much bringing a lot of great talents and abilities to you; it's more just getting rid of all the things that block you from them. It's just a matter of being where you are and who you are—honestly, openly, purely.

You who are working with this spiritual path are moving right along. Look at the reference points four years ago, three years ago, last year, last month. Look at the reference points and then at where you are today, and you'll see your progress and growth. These things come gradually and subtly. It's not thunder and lightning and fireworks per se. It's the glory of God flowing in and through you, but in such a quiet way that you may not know it until much later. Your spiritual progress started back at some point when you said, "Father, help me. Help me get through these things." And He answered.

The Only "Business" of MSIA Is Soul Transcendence

There is only one method that will set you free and that is Soul Transcendence, to live here and discover the higher reality, to extend into that greater consciousness of Light, of love, of Sound—to be that. And to overcome this level, you must go into the level that can overcome it. That level is already within you. That level is the Soul. This is why MSIA teaches moving into Soul consciousness and then into Soul Transcendence, having a life in heaven before you die and knowledge that there are greater glories all around you right now.

The Traveler does not teach reincarnation. He teaches liberation: off the planet now, for good. And before you embodied, you intended to become more aware and to use this level to bring yourself into God consciousness, to leave this land of reflected Light and enter into the ultimate, and then to take the next step as it is presented to you, for you.

So when you become tired of playing the games of negativity, the games of jealousy and anger and greed and desire, you'll turn to the greater reality of who you are and go on about the business of inner spiritual awareness. And Soul Transcendence is where the Traveler comes in and says, "Okay, let's go. Don't waste your time in the lower realms. Don't worry about the body; it's okay and takes care of itself. Don't worry about the emotions; you only need the essence of love. Don't worry about the mind; you only need the intellect to guide you through your experiences. Place your energy into the Soul, and we will travel into and beyond the Soul, into the 'high country.'"

The immediate result of Soul Transcendence is to rise above situations and see them in perspective. At that point, you don't have to solve anything. Your attitude shifts as you attune yourself to the Spirit within, and the "problem" dissolves. It's called releasing karma, and it is also called living free. As you rise up in your consciousness, the actions of this person and that person in the world have less and less consequence in your life, and it becomes easier to let them go, to forgive them, to walk away from them— because you are walking towards the Light and towards Spirit. You are experiencing and living Soul Transcendence, and the fullness and the joy of that will overshadow all the things of this world.

You may think of Soul Transcendence as a great

phenomenon that exists way out of reach. It is not out of reach. It is right here, right now. It has no dimension, no time, no level, so it cannot be separated in any way from you at any moment. It is always present. When you turn your attention to the Soul, all other levels dissolve, and you are completely free from the bonds of the lower worlds.

So remind yourself that you can move into the higher Light, the Soul, *now*. You do not have to wait for some future time when all your problems are solved and things are perfectly smooth. The experience of the Soul is here for you right now. And when you perceive the inner glory, the Beloved, the divine self, the I Am, the alpha and omega of cosmic consciousness, God awareness—however you label it—you have touched in to who you really are.

Soul Transcendence is your heritage. Awaken to the Lord living in and through you. The Traveler's love is with you, and his heart awaits your greater awakening. And while you are here, my wish for you is to be loving, to serve God and your fellow men, to be open to all the blessings that are already yours, and never to forget that this world is not your home. Your home lies beyond the Soul realm, and you get there through Soul Transcendence.

The Work of the Mystical Traveler Is Soul Transcendence

The experience the Mystical Traveler brings to you has to do with Spirit, with God, with pure love that transcends all lower levels and lifts you into Soul—and then beyond. The experience the Traveler brings to you is Soul Transcendence.

The Traveler Consciousness offers the "shortcut" into God consciousness by direct alignment. When you've touched to the Traveler Consciousness, you've touched the supreme line of consciousness. The Traveler comes through with such a pure line of teachings that it reaches right out to the Spirit inside of you, and the teachings are imparted directly from Spirit to Spirit. That's why it works so well. It's not the Traveler's spiritual form teaching your physical form. It is a transcendent process.

When you decided that what you wanted more than anything else was to know God and your own divine nature, to know yourself as Soul, perfect and complete, you created your connection to the Mystical Traveler. And the Traveler's job with you isn't so much to teach as to share with you, give to you, and assist you to awaken to Spirit. The Traveler draws forth what is already present, the awareness of truth inside you. The Traveler presents the truth to you and supplies you with the energy that will recognize the truth. The Traveler bears witness to the Light energy inside you, not as a reflective process, but as a direct reality. And when you see the Traveler, read the Soul Awareness Discourses, listen to the seminars, or chant your initiation tone, you are involved in a direct connection and a direct process with the Traveler.

One of the Mystical Traveler's jobs is to assist you in breaking free of all the blocks that stand between you and your full and complete awareness of the Soul level and the freedom of the Soul. One of the values that the Mystical Traveler brings forward is not so much the keys for making this life on Earth work for you (although sometimes that consciousness can illuminate aspects of your life more clearly than you ever thought possible), but the knowledge of the higher dimensions of Light. If you are an initiate, the Traveler's contract with you is to establish you in the consciousness of Soul. You can trust that like you trust the sun coming up. It will hold until it is completed.

And when you are working with the Traveler, all things unfold in their right and proper timing. You can assist by loving yourself every step of the way, by doing your spiritual exercises to gain a greater perspective of what you are experiencing, by loving the people around you and treating them with kindness, and by living with integrity and honesty.

The Mystical Traveler works with you only in a state of invitation and agreement. You must ask the Traveler to be with you and to work with you, and you must agree to its presence in your life. The invitation and agreement must be made every day, every moment. Each day, you must ask anew for the Traveler to be present with you, and doing spiritual exercises is one of the most effective ways of asking for the Traveler to be a part of your life.

What the Traveler does, he does from loving. Even when he brings correction and holds you to your responsibility, he does it from loving. It may not always sound that way at first, but it is the motivation behind the action. When people come up to the one anchoring the Traveler Consciousness, that consciousness is immediately awake, alive, aware, and active, relating and loving with them. It sometimes brings a balm of soothing to them, if that is what they need. It sometimes brings a kick in the pants, if they need that. It is perfect loving, whatever the expression. The Traveler brings each person exactly what is needed for them to change and lift into greater freedom.

Of course, at the moments when the drama and romance

are being undermined, you often don't like it very much and don't see it as part of your upliftment. The Traveler knows you don't see it. That's okay; he does it anyway because he has said he will get you to the Soul level. And he'll do that.

All your dilemmas and romance, your suffering and confusion, will be dissolved instantaneously if you just give it all to the Traveler Consciousness in your moments of meditation, contemplation, quietness, and spiritual exercises. But you must also give up the memory or you will pull it right back on top of you. So dispense with your suffering. Give it away. Give it to the Traveler; he will take it. But you have to let it go. You can't give it and hang on to it at the same time. The Traveler will trade you: give him your suffering, and he will give you your next step in progression; give him your darkness, and you'll see the Light appear in your consciousness. Then watch for the upliftment to appear.

The Traveler just shares himself with those who are his beloveds, those who are the initiates. The Traveler does not offer only an association; the Traveler offers a relationship that abides in the spiritual heart, nowhere else. It is a relationship of living love. And when the Traveler talks to you, he talks to the Soul. The Traveler speaks loving. It is love. It will lift you in love.

Since the Traveler comes in on love, move to love, and

you'll find the Traveler entirely present in your heart. You'll feel the Traveler behind your eyes, sharing your world with you. You'll sense the Traveler walking beside you, touching your hand, as you walk down the street. As you move to that quiet place inside, you'll feel the Traveler's embrace and know that you and the Traveler are one. So place your love in the heart of the Traveler. That is living love. Everything, even your breathing, becomes loving. Your touch becomes loving. Your whole approach becomes loving. Then everything you do, you do for love.

The Traveler Is Closer to You Than Your Breath

The Traveler is always with you. All you need to do is attune yourself to the loving you share and follow as the Traveler leads you home to the heart of God. And you will never know the Traveler truly if you know him only physically. To know the Traveler, you must awaken him in your heart. You are already awake in the Traveler's heart. Now you must awaken the Traveler in yours. He is there waiting, and in that loving place, you and he are one.

The Mystical Traveler's work is whatever the work is inside of you because you're also the Mystical Traveler. It doesn't take my physical body to tell you that. It takes you doing spiritual exercises, tuning in, and finding out, "My God, I am this, also." And you'll have the same information that I have. Then it depends upon your level of loving how you might use it.

But when you neglect your spiritual exercises, you may not feel the presence of the Traveler, so you may think the

Traveler has deserted you. It hasn't. You just haven't been focusing on the Spirit within and the Traveler's presence, so you probably think it's gone. All you have to do is turn inside to find that the Traveler never went anywhere. It's always with you, it's always present, and all you have to do is turn towards the Traveler. He never leaves you, so you'll always find him as soon as you look.

If you go through a difficult situation, the Traveler goes through it with you. Sometimes he sits in a chair, experiencing the same pain that you're experiencing in your back, leg, stomach, or wherever, even though you may be a hundred miles or three thousand miles from him physically. The Traveler goes through it with you, and it works with you to get you free of that. These things don't happen once in a while; they happen twenty-four hours a day. And if you will go in to the Inner Master, the Traveler can clear out-of-balance situations with you faster because he can work them off in the inner consciousness without being disturbed in the physical body. The Traveler does these things because he loves you, and he will do them to get you through these levels and beyond these levels into Soul consciousness.

The next big step is for your loving to come forward so you recognize the Traveler as you. So reach out and embrace the Traveler in your inner awareness. Know that form as the essence of yourself, your Inner Master, which is closer to you than your breath, more real than any other level. Know that in the Traveler's love, you will walk straight into the heart of God and awaken to the pure form of God's beingness within you.

My love is always with you. Use it to lift and sustain yourself until you know for yourself your own divinity.

Initiation into the Sound Current of God

Students in MSIA are initiated through the Mystical Traveler Consciousness into the Sound Current, the audible stream of energy that comes from the heart of God. To be an initiate of the Traveler is to devote yourself to the God within you, to Spirit, and to returning to your home, the Soul realm, from which you originally came before you incarnated onto this earth.

Your connection to Spirit through your initiation is more valuable than anything else in existence. The initiatory tone is the direct link between your consciousness and the Sound Current of God, and it is one of the greatest keys to your spiritual freedom that exists. You are placing yourself in the mainstream of Sound that is flowing back into the Supreme Godhead. It is the ultimate prayer and will bring with it the ultimate fulfillment.

And when you are devoted to the Sound and the Light, you are devoted to that consciousness which is the Traveler,

you are devoted to yourself, and you are devoted to each
other.

The Only Wrong Way to Do S.e.'s Is Not to Do Them

Spiritual exercises (s.e.'s) are designed to awaken you to the Soul. They provide the Soul with a vehicle through which it may come more fully present in this environment. In that respect, they are like no other activity in this physical, material world, and no other activity replaces spiritual exercises. S.e.'s have been designed not by the Traveler, but by Spirit, which says, "This is the way set up to reach Me. There will be various ones who will keep coming forward with that message. They are the direct representative of the Sound Current." Through the Light and Sound of God, true knowledge is available.

Spiritual exercises are an attunement with the loving quality, the pure loving that exists between you and God, and when you chant the sacred names of God, you more directly pull energy from Spirit to yourself. The spiritual consciousness is already there. Doing s.e.'s strengthens your awareness so that you may see Spirit through spiritual eyes.

Through doing s.e.'s, you also create a channel, an opening, a tunnel, through which Spirit can convey Its wisdom to you. Your job is to separate fiction and reality and discern which is which. S.e.'s will help you to discern the levels more clearly. They give you a chance to become quiet and to allow the spiritual experience to lift you so you become defined as something greater than the physical experience. And if you find yourself caught up in negative or addictive patterns of behavior, the remedy often is to get off by yourself, do a lot of s.e.'s , and rebuild your reserves.

As you consciously learn to hold increased energy within yourself during your spiritual exercises, you will be able to ride the energy higher and higher as it thrusts out with even greater power. Part of the action of doing s.e.'s is to be able to leave your body under your own volition and travel through the upper realms of consciousness so that you can get higher than the level you are presently on and see it more clearly.

If you look at this physical level through your emotions, mind, or unconscious, you see it through the distortions of those levels, but if you can get higher and see this level from the Soul level, you can have a much greater understanding of the reality of what you are perceiving. S.e.'s can activate the truth inside you and give you the thrust to act and effect change in your life. The Soul energy floods down from the higher levels into the physical and gives you the energy to move. So do spiritual exercises so you can lift above the mundane activities of your life and see how you are working things out and learning the lessons that are important to you. Then you can love yourself even though you may have made some mistakes along the way.

Still, spiritual exercises are not *designed* to smooth your way in this world. They are not designed for you to practice only until things are the way you want them. They are designed to move you through the realms of Light until you reach God. Nor are s.e.'s the goal. They are the means to achieve the goal. The goal is Soul awareness or God awareness. The value in spiritual exercises is that you make the Spirit familiar to you so that you can replace the familiarity of the world's distractions, activities, and excitements with the familiarity of the Spirit inside.

So if you would know the fullness of Spirit, make your life one gigantic spiritual exercise. Commit yourself to yourself, every moment. It's the most valuable thing you can do. Dedicate yourself to yourself, and make this dedication first priority, whether you're in a relationship, a marriage, a demanding career, or any other situation. Your first priority is to your own spiritual awakening. And every time you do s.e.'s, it becomes Christmas season. It becomes the Festival of Lights. It becomes the words of the prophets of old. All the scriptures become alive because you're walking with God.

The Teachings Are Inside

It's important to keep in mind that the outer teachings will never be as dynamic or pure as the inner teachings. It is the Traveler that resides within you who continuously—every moment of every day—gives you the spiritual message from God that you are in your purest form. The person who is truly working within the Movement of Spiritual Inner Awareness goes within to get the answers from the Mystical Traveler, the Inner Master.

Keep in mind, also, that God dwells within you, as you; all you need do is awaken to His presence, and one way to do that is to listen within yourself to His loving direction. Ask for God's will to be manifested through you, and then listen for God's voice to speak in your spiritual heart. You have to go inside and talk with the one who is illuminated and enlightened. You keep talking, keep listening, keep communicating, and keep exercising your awareness.

There are no secrets within you. There is no solution

that is hidden from you. There is nothing kept back. All wisdom is available to you at every moment. It is your challenge and your responsibility to attune yourself to Spirit and to the God within so that you may receive the wisdom from yourself. So look inward for your direction. Go to the true self, which has all knowledge. It will direct you and guide you.

Check It Out for Yourself

Be true to your inner guidance, which is your loving speaking to you and leading you. But never follow blindly the guidance you receive. Check it out. That way, you learn to trust yourself, for you are the only one who can validate your own truth and wisdom. How do you build up the knowledge of God's inner guidance? By spiritual exercises. By practicing. By moving on the guidance you receive, checking the results, continually refining the attunement, and being honest with yourself.

This inner guidance you may receive from Spirit within can sound alien and strange to you if you haven't listened to it for "centuries," yet it is that small voice in the wilderness of your spiritual heart that is telling you the truth. It's saying, "I am the Beloved. I am the one for whom you have been searching. I am the God that dwells in your heart." You awaken to that voice through spiritual exercises, through contemplation, and by taking the time to be with yourself, away from the distractions and confusions of the world.

The words written in this book may not solve your problems for you. They may not solve anything at all. They may give you some guidelines and directions that will assist *you* in solving your own problems. If anything at all is required, it's just that you check these things out for yourself. Observing is another way of saying "check it out." So observe, be your own scientific investigator, and see what results you discover.

You must check me out. You must check out my teachings. I've never told anybody to believe me or trust me. That would be nonsense and would be tempting you to your downfall. I am not at all concerned whether you believe what I tell you. If you want to know the truth, you will check it all out for yourself. You will meditate upon the teachings, asking God and the Holy Spirit to show you what is true. No one can really teach you; you teach yourself. People who have greater awareness can point out the teachings to you and declare them to you and affirm them to you, but in the last analysis, they'll say, "Now, you have to decide for yourself." So you must test the teachings to find out if they are true and valid for *you*. When you hear any teaching or message, you should always test it out.

So work the new ideas that come your way. See what they do. You won't be deceived by anyone if you check things out thoroughly. Just because the Traveler says something to you doesn't mean for one minute that you have to follow or believe it. Something inside of you may be saying, "So far, he's always told me the truth," and that's the moment you truly have to watch because the next moment could be a pitfall. Prove to yourself what the Traveler tells you or forget it.

And if you think the Traveler told you something inwardly, before doing it, look at it to make sure it's for the highest good, physically and spiritually. Lean into it, and use your intelligence to evaluate the pros and cons. If you're still not sure, you can write to the Traveler and ask. Most of you will be able to discern the truth by the time you finish writing the letter. You can then burn the letter and go on about living a Light-filled life. And if you're still unsure, remember this: when in doubt, don't do; when in doubt, talk it out.

Get Your Own Experience

Faith and belief are nice, but they are no substitute for the knowledge based on your own experience, which validates your beingness.

Putting a rain almanac on the wall and trying to squeeze rain out of it will never work, but some people take sacred scripture and try to squeeze Spirit out of it, and that doesn't work either. We get water and food by the direct experience, not by any type of vicarious fulfillment; we also get spiritual essence by direct experience. You will know what I'm saying only when you experience it. The words can appeal to the intellect and may keep your mind happy. The words may also be worthless to you until you can use them to transcend the mind and step into higher consciousness.

Opinions Are Like Noses

Opinions are like noses: everybody has one. You wouldn't live in someone's nose, so why live in their opinion? Just because someone says something, this does not make it so. It is so only when it's so inside of you, so check things out.

And don't insist that other people live your opinion. Let them do things the way they want.

If It Works for You, Use It; If Not, Have the Wit to Let It Go

Those of us who work in the Light could be called scientists in that we test the information we receive to see if it will work. If it does work, we can use it. If it doesn't work, we can let it go.

In MSIA, we move our consciousness. That's why we call this the *Movement* of Spiritual Inner Awareness: we're moving our consciousnesses from one point to another, always seeking that which will work for us. When a point of consciousness no longer works for us, we hope we will have the wit to move to one that does. We say, also, that you must follow your own path to enlightenment, and on this inner journey, you will find that you are the only one who can decide what is right for you. You become responsible for yourself and to yourself, and to no others. You are the only one who can answer whether or not what you are doing is best for you.

So if you bow down and worship what the Traveler

tells you without trying it out, you're playing the fool. I can't say it enough times: check out everything for yourself. Don't give over your control to *anyone*. Certainly, you can listen to what other people say, walk out into life, put it into practice in a small way, and see if it works. If it does, great; move into it a little more and see if it keeps on working. Use it as long as it works. When it doesn't, keep on walking.

As you learn to tune in to your true self, you will know within yourself whether what you are doing is right for you. And you are the only one to whom you have to give an answer. If you are doing whatever you are doing to the best of your ability and striving as honestly as you can to take care of yourself, you'll find out what works for you and what does not. That will be your guideline.

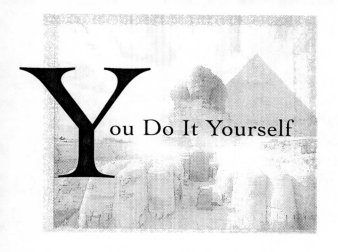

You Do It Yourself

Someone once asked me, "I'd like to know about MSIA. I'd like to know what its services are and what it will do for me." My answer was, "It will do absolutely nothing for you. There are no services that it renders. Everything you get is what you put into it. If you do your part, you'll receive back in full measure, and no one will be able to take it away from you."

In MSIA, we work with you on whatever level you're capable of working. We assist you wherever you let us, but we don't do it for you. The Traveler won't do it for you because that would stop you. You learn by doing. Some people learn rapidly and go on; others, by the nature of their conditioning, have to look closely at what's happening. They may think they are dragging their feet, but they are really moving forward in the way that's fine for them.

You don't get things in Spirit because you think you ought to have them; you get them because you work for them. The grace of the Traveler is extended to you and will assist you, and you must still do the work yourself. The Traveler is here to support you, love you, show you the way, and help you when you fall down. He will do everything he can to assist you, but he won't do it for you. You have to build up your own inner support system and keep it activated.

Red Socks, Blue Socks — You Decide

Ten percent of your consciousness is on the physical level, and 90 percent of your consciousness is on the other levels (astral, causal, mental, etheric, Soul, etc.). And in the 90 percent is where the Traveler does his work with you. Something that is in the 10-percent level is a physical-level situation and is for you to decide about. This means that with jobs, health, money, relationships, places to live, foods to eat, where to travel—whether you wear red socks or blue socks—the decisions are yours. You (and everyone) have come to this planet to learn and grow, and the Traveler won't take those learning opportunities from you, so he leaves it up to you to handle your own 10-percent level. The Traveler's work is to give you strength in the Spirit and in the Soul, so that when you have balanced the physical level, the way will be prepared to lift you into higher consciousness.

You are a spiritual being, an extension of God, yet you

also reside in a "negative" realm and must deal with a physical body, emotions, mind, and unconscious, so there are bound to be paradoxes because the physical level is one of trial and error and change. But as you become more balanced in both your inner and outer expressions, your life will become more balanced. The physical level becomes balanced as you find yourself eating better foods and monitoring how much you put in your mouth. Your emotions become balanced as you learn to love yourself and take care of yourself first and to do those things that bring you joy and fulfillment. The mental area becomes balanced as you learn to think positive thoughts and to communicate more clearly with yourself and others. Keeping these levels in balance is part of your responsibility.

You take care of your responsibilities so you're not a burden to anyone, on any level, and so you will be free to travel the high realms. You can lift yourself into a greater awareness of Spirit and God's love and still be very practical in your daily life. The two are not in conflict. You can say, "I do want Soul consciousness, and I do want to move into the higher levels. That is my goal and my deepest desire. I am also here in this world today, and I have to work to pay the rent." So you set your goals high and keep focused on them as you keep walking through this level. That's the way to get where you want.

Take care of yourself by being the best you can possibly

be. Live your life with the greatest integrity, the greatest loving, the greatest honesty of which you are capable. If you find yourself slipping in one of those areas, face it and take the steps necessary to clear and balance it.

And if you perceive an area in which you seem to be blocked, use the Traveler Consciousness to bring clarity and understanding. If this is an area that can be released and dissolved, the Traveler Consciousness will do it if you ask. If this is an area that is necessary for you to complete and you ask for it to be dissolved, you may gain greater understanding of why you are working in that area. The Traveler will not dissolve the area if doing that is not for your highest good, but it will assist you with the understanding.

You are of God regardless of what you do or don't do physically, so be careful not to base your evaluation of your spiritual growth upon whether you buy a new car, go into a new business, move from New York to Los Angeles, get married, or quit your job. And if you don't "see" any progress in some of your 10-percent areas, don't worry. You can't necessarily equate spiritual progress with the experiences in this world. When you look at total reality from a high point of spirituality, when you are working with the Mystical Traveler Consciousness, what you do in your physical body has very little, if anything, to do with your spiritual progression.

Remember, too, that it is the spiritual levels that are perfect; it is the Soul that is perfect. There's no perfection on the physical level, so don't worry about attaining perfection because none of us will ever be perfect here, although we can shoot for excellence. Also keep in mind that each of us is still evolving, changing, and growing, and part of our growth process involves making mistakes and making corrections.

The Traveler doesn't ask a lot of you. He asks you to do your spiritual exercises every day, to love one another, and to live without hurting yourself or others, in ways that will nurture and care for yourself and others. Within those parameters, all the choices are yours, so choose love as much as you can. These are the actions of love: increase your Light, continue your development, be a joy to everyone you see, lift yourself continually. And if there is no loving in what you're doing, you're on the wrong track. If there *is* loving, joy, and a feeling of upliftment in what you're doing, then you can't go far wrong.

Don't Hurt Yourself and Don't Hurt Others

The pure and good selfish life is wanting to live life for yourself the way you see it and allowing everyone else the freedom to do that same thing. Part of your happiness is being able to stand up in your own dignity and remove yourself from a situation of which you're not a part. You don't have to apologize to anybody or do any great explanations. You can just say, "Excuse me," in politeness to the other person's consciousness, and remove yourself. If it's done in love, it will work, and when you are truly loving, you cannot hurt yourself or another.

It is your responsibility to be loving in all your relationships while not letting yourself be taken advantage of. And often the most valid reason for an action you take will be because you want to do it. It's important for everyone to have respect for this reason. It's a good one. You have the right to do something just because you want to—as long as you are not inflicting yourself on another consciousness.

In all this, always remember that the Light will not violate anyone's consciousness. If your action violates someone else's consciousness, it is not a Light action. So evaluate your actions. Do they hurt you? If they do, that's not a Light action. Do your actions hurt others? If they do, that's not a Light action. If you are not found out right away or appear to get away with it, this does not change that reality at all. On this level, you can best serve your spiritual progression by expressing lovingly towards everyone you encounter. Treat people as they deserve to be treated, as the extension of God that they are.

We are all our brothers' keepers, but not as prison keepers. We keep our brothers free by allowing them the individual experience of their own lives, the way they see it. When you can allow people to express their Light their own way, to fulfill their destiny and walk the path to the drummer they hear, then you are, in essence, doing the same thing God does—allowing them the freedom of their expression.

Take Care of Yourself So You Can Help Take Care of Others

Your primary responsibility on this planet is to take care of yourself and to rise to your highest potential. As you become more aware spiritually, it's also important to maintain the integrity of this physical level, which means not only taking care of the physical body but also maintaining yourself financially, emotionally, and mentally. You cannot give up your responsibility to any level.

Specifically, taking care of yourself first might mean to get a job, pay your bills, take the dog for a walk, keep your house clean, or get enough sleep at night. When these basic levels are taken care of, you can then look around you to see if there are others who need help. If you are volunteering your time for this, that, and the other thing but you don't have your rent paid for this month, you really haven't been taking care of yourself first, and it may cause tension or conflict inside you. Many times, the pressures of the world are just pressures that you've put upon yourself, and they can be relieved by taking a more realistic look at your life and how you are using your time and energies.

Know, too, that there is nothing wrong with being selfish. Eating and getting proper rest are selfish for the body, thinking nice thoughts is selfish for the mind, feeling good is selfish for the emotions, and doing spiritual exercises to rouse the Soul that may be sleeping is selfish for the Spirit. Those are all healthy activities. If other people fit in with your plan for taking care of yourself, that can be fantastic. If they undermine the plan, let them go their own way. Let them go in love, with good thoughts and good feelings towards them, but let them go if they do not support you in those things that are good for you.

You can start finding your own divine love when you start loving others, but that doesn't count until you can love yourself. Should you love others more than you love yourself? No, because it is through loving yourself unconditionally that you enter into the Spirit that resides within you. That's when you become a real joy to be around. That's when you discover the Soul. When you are taking care of yourself on all levels, it becomes very easy to move into the Soul level as that opportunity presents itself. And if you want to release yourself from incarnation patterns, start assuming responsibility immediately, in this moment.

So love the physical level, maintain it, and enhance it in every way you can. Bring joy and happiness into the emotions. Keep yourself balanced and your expression loving. Think uplifting thoughts; speak kindly of others. Keep yourself clear; don't criticize or even discuss others. Hold good feelings and thoughts in your mind so you can share that goodness with other people. When they are down, help lift them by just being you. When you use this approach as a method, it becomes a way of life. If you did that from now on, you could help to create a wind that would clean the planet.

Use Everything for Your Upliftment, Learning, and Growth

The Traveler shows you the direction and walks with you into your awakening. Everything supports your doing this—every experience, every person you meet, every place you go. There is no situation that cannot lift you and point the way into your experience of the presence of God.

If you could perceive the Traveler's presence in your depression, doubt, and fear, why would you ever want to move from those? The feelings of separation and loneliness can be *tools* that move you out of your negativity and motivate you to find a more positive expression. As you lift yourself into a place of greater love and understanding, you'll feel the presence of Spirit move back into your life, and that can give you the motivation to maintain the loving quality in your life.

You come to the physical world to gain the experience that the high self is bringing forward for the Soul's evolvement. Each experience becomes your state of knowledge and beingness. And when you are secure in your knowledge of God's love for you, you know that *everything* that happens is to lift you and move you closer to your own divinity. One day, you will wake up and find yourself living in the heart of God, and you will know that all your experiences were but rungs on the ladder that led to God. So use everything in the world—all the prayers, all the books, all the Discourses, all the seminars, everything—to reflect the Spirit inside of you. Use everything as a reflection to show you the glory of your Spirit and God's glory.

There truly are no mistakes, only experiences, and you can garner a lesson from everything that happens. So don't ever berate yourself for what you see as your failures. Recognize them as areas in which you can gain more experience. Focus on your successes, however small or large they may be; they are your steps forward and upward on your spiritual path. And you can take an inward stance of, "I make mistakes, I allow myself to make mistakes, and, furthermore, I give myself permission to learn from my mistakes. Therefore, I am in a constant state of growth and evolution."

Spirit brings all experiences to you for your greater and greater awakening. Your marital problem is your gift from Spirit to bring you into Spirit. Even your broken back, your bad legs, your deformity, or the corruption of your emotions is only Spirit placing the awareness with you that will turn you back towards Spirit. And everything that happens to you is designed to strengthen and lift you—*everything!* Nothing is meant to rip you apart or hurt you in any way. When you catch that vision and know the reality of it, you won't allow anything to hurt you because how you experience it is all under your control. When something happens that you think could hurt you, just look for the blessings and discover how you can lift from the experience and use it to your advantage, because even the "negative" experiences are gifts from Spirit to build your strength, your awareness, your empathy, and your loving. Do not curse what appears to be your trouble or suffering. Thank God for it.

You can use suffering much like the gas gauge in your car. The closer your gas gauge moves towards empty, the more negative feedback you have about the fact that your car is running out of gas. You can use suffering as a "gas gauge" to show how far you are from being fully in your spiritual center. So when something happens that appears to hurt you, rather than resisting it and pushing it away, you will embrace it. You will expand your consciousness to encompass the changes and the new situation and to find what new freedoms are available to you.

When you experience negative feedback, you can just say, "Oh, yes, that taught me this," and let it go. It's like yesterday's four thousandth breath. Do you know which breath that was? Heavens, no. You've let it go. It was inconsequential to you, and that's the way all things become. You keep coming to right now. Here. Watching. When you get out of the past, you can use all the errors, all the mistakes, all the learning, all the everything as your "fertilizer" for greater growth; you can use it all to lift you.

It's also important to understand that growing is not necessarily equated with having a smooth week. You can be making forward, positive progress while you are feeling bad or experiencing confusion. Your accurate perception of what is really going on may be overshadowed at any moment by the negative aspects of your mind and emotions. But we all get things the way that we get them, and if it's through some pain and confusion and turmoil, then it's that way. It is the value received that is the important thing.

But when you curse and complain, you place negatively conditioned energy around you, and you get negativity. When you bless, love, and use everything that comes your way for your upliftment, learning, and growth, you bring positive, loving, supportive experiences into your field of energy. You can't miss. It's a natural result.

There is a Spirit inside of you watching out for you and taking care of you, no matter what. Something that looks like your greatest catastrophe is really your greatest blessing, because it will lift you into the next level of awareness. So when things happen that may seem unfair at first glance, look for the loving lesson underneath. If you can't see it there, put it there yourself so that you see everything that happens to you through the eyes of loving.

 Stumbling Blocks into Stepping-Stones

I really don't look at anything as a problem. I look at everything as an experience that comes my way so I can perceive the relationship between me and the experience and then, by learning to handle the experience, create an advantage out of it. As I do this, every experience becomes my stepping-stone.

If you look at your life this way, the "failure" of one experience can prepare you for the success of the next, and success can often be letting go of those things that block the experience of love. To move forward in your love and your spiritual progression, all you need to do is make the most out of every situation, regardless of what it is. Use everything to grow and to learn. Use every stumbling block as a stepping-stone.

Health, Wealth, and Happiness, Prosperity, Abundance, and Riches, Loving, Caring, and Sharing, and Touching to Others

In MSIA, we have nine ideas that we use in relationship to other people and ourselves: health, wealth, happiness, prosperity, abundance, riches, loving, caring, and sharing. There is also a tenth one: reaching out and touching to others and sharing all this with them. We are the only organization on the face of the planet that has all of these things as our guiding light.

Health

Health can be found in loving who you are. So take good care of yourself, which is another way to love yourself. Eat good foods. Exercise. Do those things that keep you healthy. Put your physical choices and activities in a higher perspective so you see them as opportunities to love yourself more fully.

Wealth

Being attached to the accumulation of material wealth might be a deterrent to discovering the more spiritual aspects of yourself. But material wealth can also be an outer reflection of the inner wealth and abundance that you are experiencing inside. There is nothing "wrong" with having material possessions. Sometimes they can assist you to live a more comfortable life so that you can more easily be of service to others. And many times sharing the abundance of your material possessions can be beneficial to others. It's all in how you handle it inside yourself.

Happiness

Happiness is inherent in the consciousness of Soul and can only be realized by traveling the inner path. The illusion in your endless outward seeking is that the true self has been beguiled by the world, and you are out there searching in the world to find your happiness. So be careful that you don't give away to the whims of the outer world your ability to create and experience joy within yourself. When you move to the power source of your beingness in the inner kingdom, you find happiness and joy, which is the nature of who you are. It is a dynamic joy, an active expression of happiness. And within that happiness is peace. It may not be a jovial or raucous happiness, but it is one where the warmth of your own consciousness is united with the knowingness of your Soul. And when those two aspects are one, happiness is the natural result.

Prosperity

Prosperity is for you—both the abundance of Spirit and the manifestation on this physical level. So make a choice to choose prosperity, to focus on it, and to decide that not only do you deserve it but you're going to go for it and get it. And if you create an attitude of supporting yourself and others in doing the best you and they can, many aspects of creating your prosperity and abundance can fall into line.

Abundance

It has been said, "You are all gods. You are all abundant. You are all creators." As you know this and experience the joy of being part of this, you can experience the ease of creating abundance, sharing it, and creating even greater abundance, as an ongoing, replenishing process, all in the perfect timing of Spirit. And since Spirit is a constantly expansive, available energy that is dynamically present, it is up to each individual to keep the channel open to receive of the blessings of abundance.

Riches

Riches may represent dollars, but they might not. It may be that you are rich in friends. Or your riches may be in your health, in your family, in your society. And nothing is as good as health, as the wealth of health and the happiness of health. When you hit that, the riches of the world mean nothing. Jesus said it this way: "Do not store up for yourselves treasures on earth, where moth and rust destroy, and where thieves break in and steal. But store up for yourselves treasures in heaven, where moth and rust do not destroy, and where thieves do not break in and steal" (Matthew 6:19, 20).

Loving

What matters in each and every moment is that you are loving. Be loving to yourself and to others. When you are doing that, in the reality of each moment, all other dilemmas will fall into line, and you will begin attuning yourself to the greater love that is the love of the Traveler. The first step is to be loving. It is also important to understand that you probably won't get an advantage over anyone in this world by having an open, loving heart. All that is going to happen is that you will live in a higher state of consciousness while you walk through the lower levels. That's it. And that's enough.

Caring

There is a great field of loving that moves through the people who are united in the Traveler's love. It's manifested through each one of you as you are caring, helping, working, and just being friendly with one another. And the way to tell if you're really being friendly to other people is the heartfelt response that is truly caring for them.

Sharing

You never know all of God's plan, so don't miss any opportunity to tell someone of the love of your beingness and the love of God's beingness. But don't cram it down their throats or make them feel that they don't have love or that they're not worthwhile. Live in the love of your own beingness and share that with others, for there is nothing quite as nice as sharing your loving heart. A little loving can awaken others to their own Light, and then they, in turn, can share it with more people. We can change the world this way.

Touching to Others

The Light of your consciousness is the most magnificent gift that you can ever give, the most valuable thing there is. Your individual expression of the Light is so precious in its perfection and beauty, and the Light in you will attract the Light in others. Don't be afraid to take someone's hand. Don't be afraid to hug people. Share the love. Give it out. The love will be greater in you as a result.

Our challenge is to take what we've learned and share it. If we don't share what we've learned, if we don't reach out and share our experience with others, then there is very little value in our having participated. What we're dealing with is the overall upliftment of society—the actual transformation of the planet. That transformation is possible if we are willing to reach out, if we're willing to communicate, to share, and to touch those people in our lives.

My Prayer

Lord God, as You've always heard me, as You've always talked to me, see if You can see it clear to talk to the hearts of these who are Your people that are choosing You. Sustain them in what they plant. Let them reap the harvest. Let them have the abundance, prosperity, and riches, the health, wealth, and happiness, the loving and the caring. But mostly, Lord, let them involve themselves in the sharing.

Karma Is Spelled S.T.U.P.I.D.

Karma is the inability to change an action or to act differently. People have asked me, "How do I know what my karma is?" I say, "What do you do all or most of the time?" They'll tell me and I'll say, "That's your karma." If they say, "But I do other things," I tell them, "Well, there's more than one karma."

Karma is also stupid. It just doesn't have any working intellect at all. You step away from your karma by exercising your intelligence, your positive direction, and your integrity. If you're in a situation that is not working for you, that is bringing you imbalance and pain and confusion, you have the right to set your course in another direction and move away from that which is not working.

Put simply, karma is "as you sow, you reap." Things come back to you that you set in motion a long, long time ago. When you're working directly with the Traveler, you have the opportunity to clear the karma not only of this life but also of previous times. You have the opportunity to finish up in this lifetime and walk free. It's a great opportunity and a great blessing. As you walk through the karma, however, it can appear to be very strange. Your challenge is to maintain the focus of Spirit, Light, and Sound and just keep moving steadily forward in that direction, no matter what is happening around you.

If you're smart and wise, the karma that you create during the day, you disperse by the end of the night. If you take a negative thought over to the next morning, you are on the way to building more karma. This is why we say, don't go to bed with things "hanging on your head." Get up and write them on a piece of paper and burn it, if you have to. If you could call up a person and say, "Look, I misrepresented myself and I just want to square it," you'd be further ahead.

And if some people continually evoke a negative response within you, you can put these people in the Light, knowing full well that they are not responsible for how you feel. *You* are responsible for your response. It then becomes so much easier because you cannot hate anyone or push them away. You can't hate them because they are helping you to balance your past actions, to become clearer, and to lift your consciousness.

The protection of the Mystical Traveler is spiritual, not necessarily physical. If a karmic action can be handled in the night travels rather than in the physical, then it may well be that you don't have to go through the action physically. If it is for your highest good for you to go through an action physically, then you will go through it. So don't assume anything; pay attention to what you do here and don't get yourself into situations where it is obvious that there is potential for physical harm.

Love your karma. It is your opportunity to learn and gain wisdom, and you have the opportunity to change the karmic flow of your life through your ability to be loving. By loving the God in yourself and others, you can move into a path of greater unfoldment. Through loving, you can complete your karma.

And don't be shocked at or condemn yourself for how unaware you've been for years. When the veil is parted and you see spiritually, you may see many of the imbalances you've created. As a result, you could enter into condemnation unless you keep the spiritual door open and continually receive the flow of grace, the divine consciousness. When you can do that, you may clear all those past imbalances.

When this body falls away, the Spirit-form that will be you will not have any of the personality things pulling on it. So right now, pull up inside of you. Bless your exterior senses. Bless what you see. Bless the food you eat. Bless the bodies you touch. Be thankful for the clothing you have.

Have compassion upon this planet; it's in need of it, but it can have compassion only from someone who carries compassion. You carry compassion. Exercise it through your senses, and you walk through it karmically free.

The Loyal Forces of the Opposition

I call the negative power "the loyal forces of the opposition," since its job is to make sure we learn our lessons so that we can go back into the higher spiritual realms. It does much to strengthen us, and in this way it can be seen as positive.

The loyal forces of the opposition are going to make sure that you are worthy of any new position you assume. They are going to make sure that you just don't *think* you know. They're going to make sure that you don't just go on faith. You're going to have to *know* and be able to accomplish what you say you can; you are going to have to experience, demonstrate, and manifest the Soul consciousness.

The negative power will come against you because its job is to make sure you become as strong as you can through the experiences of this world. Its prime directive is to distract you into the world so that you don't do the things that will build the energy sufficiently to thrust you through to Soul consciousness. And as you get higher, the distractions become much more subtle. If you follow the direction of any negative form, it will become your focus, so be careful because the negative power is very smart, and its lessons are not necessarily loving or uplifting.

In MSIA, we do not pay a lot of attention to the negative power, though we do learn how to hold a focus of loving in the face of it, because we keep our attention on where we are going—Soul Transcendence and God.

We Are All One

It can be a beautiful, beautiful world when you realize that the divine essence that is *you* is also within everyone else. When you cannot accept and love one person, you create separation towards everyone. You also create a separation between you and the God in you and between you and the God in everyone. But it's easy to see a portion of God rolling up in front of you in everything that you see. So you look for the divine in everything and everyone.

The very first MSIA Discourse says that MSIA teaches the brotherhood of man and the Fatherhood of God. Love is the bond that creates the brotherhood. And love will set you free to discover the Fatherhood of God. So stand up in the beingness of your own love, and let that love be your connection to all things. In personal relationships, you give and take and share. You lift one another, knowing that the one consciousness is the consciousness that's flooding through all, in various levels of awareness. You must also be able to take the special love you have for a close friend or spouse and, in the spiritual quality of that love, give it to *everyone* who comes into your presence.

When you recognize that we are all one, you will also know that if you hurt another, you hurt yourself. So you will—automatically—love and bless each one you meet. You will—automatically—forgive any action and seek to relieve any process of guilt that might appear in yourself or anyone else, so that no one will be delayed on your account.

There is truly only one Beloved: the God-form. You are part of it. Everyone is. When you look to the Beloved, you separate and create two where there is only one, but we are one in God's loving heart, and there is only the Beloved. So let yourself know the closeness and the fellowship of the Beloved within you, and know that the apparent differences you perceive on the outer are only different reflections of the same inner essence. We walk through this life with God beside us as our guide. We are never alone, never separated, always loved and cared for. We are in God's heart. And the larger your spiritual heart becomes and the more you live in the center of your spiritual heart, the more you'll discover that you are awake in the heart of all the world.

Everyone Is Doing the Best They Can with What They Know

If you will keep in mind that almost every person is attempting to do the best they can, you can have much more congenial relationships. And this includes you. You can say to yourself, "I am tired of saying that I can't handle things. From now on, I'm going to handle things the best way I can from where I am and with what I know, and I'm going to allow other people the same right." Ah! You are in unconditional love, unconditionally loving everyone all the time.

When people hit against me with their unkind words, I think, "God bless you. There must be so much turmoil inside of you to have to do that. It must really be difficult living with all that hurt and agony inside. So I won't do anything to make it worse for you." For if you could look at the agony, the heartache, and the sorrow of your worst enemies, you would find that they have more than they can hope to handle, and you would do nothing but send them thoughts of love and joy and happiness. You would just leave them alone with your mouth, your emotions, your mind, and your physical body. You might just ask God in His mercy to extend to them everlasting peace.

If you can't love somebody, it's best to say, "I don't know who they are." That's a clear statement because if you don't love someone, you really don't know who they are. Anyone who is truly known to you is loved. So do you love and assist those you are with? Do you keep in mind that all people are doing the best they can with what they know? Do you use the Light in all situations to assist and uplift? If that's your expression, you are moving into Soul.

Magic Words

When you are a positive power, a "lighthouse," that positiveness will go out to people. You bless every person you walk by during the day when that Light is flowing through you. When you walk by someone and, either out loud or silently, you say, "God bless you," the power of the mind will send positive energy out to that person.

I have told young people whose parents fight a lot, "When your parents are fighting, just sit or stand nearby and say over and over in your mind, 'God bless you.'" Some of the youngsters have done this and reported back that although their parents were fighting and really up-set with each other, pretty soon they just went quiet and walked away. And later they started kidding around a little bit, and everything was all right again.

There are also other magic words that create positiveness. Silently saying "God bless you" can certainly change people, but if you really want to watch them change in a hurry, silently add, "I love you." They can become absolutely elated. The negativity goes, and the positive energy sweeps in. To do even more, you can add, "Peace, be still," and extend that to all creation even in the midst of upset.

Love is a cohesive power that brings everything together. Love has the potential to change it all into positive action and a positive flow of Spirit. These magic words can cause miracles to happen.

Acceptance Is the First Law of Spirit

We talk of Spirit and the spiritual laws of acceptance, cooperation, understanding, and enthusiasm. You must first accept yourself before you can accept others, and you must first cooperate with yourself before you can cooperate with others. Acceptance does not imply belief. Acceptance implies acknowledgment of what's going on. It does not state "true" or "false"; it only acknowledges. If you accept the presence of someone in your life, you can start cooperating with that person, and that cooperation produces the *experience* that will give you the understanding. Then you can become enthusiastic within the understanding, and the enthusiasm gives you the impetus to transcend the negative levels and reach into Soul.

The reason more of us are not spiritually aware people is that we often don't or won't accept what is happening. Acceptance is a flow of consciousness that continually moves on to the next thing. So accept whatever comes your way, and don't grumble against anything that happens to you. If it happens, it happens. Go on about your business. Keep flowing. You cannot control circumstances from the outside, so instead of resisting pain or failure and defending against it, you can embrace and encompass your pain and your failures, fully accepting them so that they become part of you. You then can let them go because they are part of your inner environment—they are within your domain—and the loving of your Soul can dissolve them.

When we surrender our petty control patterns to our Soul—which is on a higher and more refined level than our minds, emotions, and bodies—we transfer our consciousness to what is really running things. We then don't have to make things happen in our lives. They simply happen, and our task is to cooperate with the natural movement inherent in all things.

So never forget that you are more than what you do. You are more than anything you teach. You are more than anything you say. You are more than anything you could ever express. Always keep in mind that the highest good will prevail and that you simply need to cooperate with it. It's ironic, but the key to being truly in control is cooperation.

When you simply let your own self, which is God, shine through, there is such freedom because you never have to pretend to be something you're not. If you're feeling particularly loving and positive, that's fine. If you're not, that's fine, too. It's okay to be whoever you are in the moment. Misery is separation and the feeling of being separated. Joy is the oneness of all. To reach the oneness, you accept and own all aspects of living: the mistakes, the glory, the deceit, and the integrity. When you accept and own it all, there is nothing you are not, and you become one with God, which is all.

The Soul Is Neutral

Neutrality is a progressive, assertive statement of your being, without attachment to results or to the processes of getting someplace. It's enough that you're there enjoying things. No matter what someone else does, you continue to express from your heart. And the more neutrality you can bring to what you observe, the more able you are to work in alignment with God's will here on the physical level.

Being neutral doesn't mean that you don't care for yourself and others. You can be loving and caring and still be neutral. Neutrality comes from a higher perspective that sees more of the total picture and realizes that the highest good may be served through ways that, at first glance, may not appear to be positive and uplifting.

Looking at things this way can help you let go more, and the idea of letting go can be fearful to a lot of people because there are things they like and enjoy in the world and in their expression. But you can let go of the *attachment* and continue the expression; that is neutral.

"Neutral" is the loving heart, which is the Soul. When the loving heart is flowing and functioning, it has no wants and desires—none. It is the emotions that want this and that. When you're neutral and unattached, you don't care what anyone else does. You do care that you're loving and open and that you're expanding your consciousness. What if it doesn't expand at the rate you want? You're not neutral as soon as you entertain that thought. You're intellectualizing and may be setting a trap for yourself. Instead of listening to the intellect, listen to your spiritual heart.

The Soul does not see things as good or bad, and it places no judgments; it is neutral. When you can more fully express that consciousness of neutrality, you will be moving towards the consciousness of the Soul. And one of the Mystical Traveler's jobs with you in this three-dimensional world is to awaken the multidimensional levels within you and to let you know that negativity is just an attitude. You become neutral when you recognize that your love is God's love and your joy is God's joy, and all you do is share—from one God to another.

Observation Is the Key to Letting Go

Observation is a matter of staying within your own spiritual center, maintaining your awareness of yourself and of the spiritual power and protection available to you, and simply watching what happens in the outer environment.

To know what is spiritual in a situation, you have to get above it, not run any of your own "stuff" on it, and move to a place of observation. If you would just enter into observation, you would be able to perceive so much more clearly. From that state of observation, you realize that there's nothing there. You have nothing to gain or lose one way or another, and it doesn't matter whether you are involved or not. You'll be able to see things really clearly, just for what they are. And if you don't see something clearly, you shouldn't assume anything about it, because as soon as you assume anything, you've moved out of observation and you have your own stuff mixed up in there.

We don't stay in this level; we go through it. We don't become a major catastrophe to ourselves when, for example, we have a fever of 101. We watch it to see what it's telling us. Sometimes it's burning out a disease in the body. Sometimes the heat of the body is destroying an unwanted virus or something like that. So don't be too anxious to change something. Watch it to see what it is telling you. You don't have to push your panic button and man the lifeboats at the first little sign of something. You just observe it.

Observation is a state of detachment that lifts you into a greater awareness, and you can become more and more free. The process of observing what is so about your life helps release you from ego and can allow the power of God to flow through you. All you have to do is open and say, "Lord, I receive. Thank You for Your presence." So thank God for all your experiences. You're here to learn. You grow into your divine potential by very carefully watching all the levels of your consciousness.

Take Mental Dominion

You cannot control the mind or the emotions, but you can direct them the way you want them to go. When the emotions flood forward, you can stand clear of those emotions. You can change your direction and place a new direction for yourself to move mentally and emotionally.

You are not responsible for what comes *into* your mind. A lot of things come into your mind all day long, and you can let any thought just flow in and flow out. You are responsible for what you *hold* in your mind and for those thoughts to which you add your energy. So be careful what you hold in your mind because you may become that.

The point is not to do away with the emotions and thoughts but to become master of them and use them, as necessary. Use them when they come in, and put them aside when you no longer need them. You can demonstrate your ability to assert and maintain dominion over your inner environment. This is the joy of being the master of the household.

There's Got to Be a Pony Here Someplace

The story is told of two little boys who were put into two rooms piled high with manure. A couple of hours went by, and someone checked on the two boys. One was crying and complaining about the sight and the smell of the manure and his "horrible" fate at being shut up in the room. The other little boy was smiling with great joy and shoveling manure just as fast as he could. When asked why he looked so happy, he said, "With all this manure, there's got to be a pony around here someplace."

You cannot control your outer environment; you can control yourself. You are the master of any situation that comes your way. You might say, for example, "Yes, but I'm going to school and the professor asks me to do certain things, and then he tests me on them. How can I be the master of that?" You are not the master of the professor; he is the master of himself, and since he is the creator of the situation, he is in control of it. You, however, are the master of yourself, and within that situation, you can control yourself.

Your job on this planet is rather well laid out for you. It is to keep your attitude, your consciousness, in a favorable condition for your self-growth. And much of your ability to open to new things, to be able to incorporate new ideas into your life, to change your patterns of behavior, and to grow depends on your attitude towards the situations in which you find yourself. If you can keep a positive attitude, you can learn from any situation. You can continually grow and lift in consciousness, and life can be a beautiful experience.

There are thousands of people studying with the Mystical Traveler who are saying, "In this freedom and love you're bringing forward—even though the situation hasn't cleared and it's still a garbage pile—I now realize it's compost. I just let a lot of things grow and use them to a great advantage." So when things are not as you would like, you can lift your attitude and look for the lesson, the good, and the blessing in your experience. If you can do that, you can turn it into something positive and gain a greater consciousness of Light.

An immediate result of Soul Transcendence is to rise above situations and see them in perspective. At that point, you don't have to solve anything. Your attitude shifts as you attune yourself to the Spirit within, and the "problem" dissolves. It's called releasing karma. And it is also called living free.

The World Is Perfect— You Just Don't Like It That Way

The Soul, which is your greatest reality, is perfect. You are already perfect in who you are and what you are. And although you may not know it yet, God's plan for you, for your neighbor, and for the world, is perfect. So if there are still areas of your life that cause you difficulty, *bless them*. Those areas are your blessings because they move you to seek the Kingdom of God. If all things were perfect here, you might forget all about your spiritual direction.

If you attach yourself to anything in the lower levels and misplace your allegiance, your loyalty, your love, it may be taken from you. And that is the greatest blessing that you may ever receive, so don't be too quick to curse those "difficulties" that befall you. They may be perfectly designed to enhance your greatest good. If all things are right and proper because God is right and proper and if all things are moving towards divine destiny, then your challenge is to see that and to work in that.

You see, these lower levels can be full of errors, frustrations, and mistakes. They're designed that way. They're designed to refine your level of awareness so you can discover more completely who you are. People ask, "What's for my highest good?" The Traveler answers, "You'll find out when you do it." Then they say, "I don't want to make a mistake. I don't want to do anything that will delay my spiritual growth." The Traveler says, "You can't. Your spiritual progress is not necessarily determined by your physical situation."

And if there are some areas of your life that may be imperfect and incompletely balanced, can you accept that those may be areas for you to learn about and experience and that perhaps you are not to receive a perfect healing and balance yet? Could it be that this is the prod that keeps you going and growing, searching and questing? Is it possible that this is set up perfectly for your highest good? The truth is that with each breath, God is saying, "I'm right here. Everything's fine." That is the eternal essence of God that is entirely present at every moment.

You're Never Given Anything You Can't Handle

Spirit will never give you anything you can't handle. So you can be assured that you will always be able to handle what is. You do that by staying present in the moment and just moving through each experience as it appears. You can handle all situations and overcome your dilemmas by moving to your center and pulling forward universal strength. As long as you keep your consciousness centered, as long as you keep yourself free of expectations and opinions of what should or should not be taking place, and as long as you let your experiences flow into you, you are lifting. At that point, no matter who you are with or where you are, you will be moving forward on your path.

And when you are an initiate of the Traveler and are working closely and consciously with Spirit, there is no need to ask for anything beyond whatever is for your highest good for your next level of unfoldment. All things are already being brought to you to lift you, to purify you, to prepare you to receive the keys of God's kingdom.

There Are No Emergencies in Spirit

It's important to remember that there are really no crises or emergencies. You're either going to live or you're going to die, and if you die, you're really going to live. So there are no emergencies or crises in Spirit. And if you're involved in what feels like an emergency or crisis, don't sit by the telephone. Sit by the Mystical Traveler Consciousness, which is not going to come across on the phone but through the Soul level.

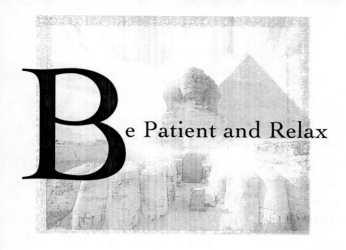

Be Patient and Relax

To "let go and let God," be patient and relax. What if, right now, God is using you to bring His Light and power into this physical-level world? What if, right now, you are living in accordance with God's plan for you? What if your feeling a little sad and lonely is a tool for you to know yourself more deeply? What if the house burning down is a way God has designed to release you from a lot of worldly attachments and lift your attention to His presence? What if all things here are designed for your greatest growth and upliftment? If you can catch that vision, it will be easier for you to let go and let God.

You cannot get away from the essence of Spirit within. If you try to deny that essence, the result is disturbance and imbalance. The butterflies in your stomach are you placing yourself against yourself. You don't need to do that. You only need to relax, to let go, and to allow the ongoing process of Spirit to take care of you. And not a single moment goes by that does not bring you the opportunity to know the Soul more deeply and more fully. You are the vehicle for experiencing and knowing your Soul. So relax, hold back nothing, and let your Soul be. When you make space for the blessings of Soul to manifest, you become a living blessing.

So give yourself time to let your life unfold within God's timing and in God's way. Trust the Spirit. Trust the Traveler within you. Let Spirit do for you what you may not have the wit to do for yourself. God takes perfect care of you, if you will only allow it, and life can be very exciting when you let go and let God, when you are patient and relax. If you push for your way, you can end up with karma. If you flow with God's will, you're free.

You Can Go Through Life Laughing or Crying

Life is just humor at its funniest state, and when something difficult happens to you, it's important to see that you must go on, regardless of your attitude. You can go on laughing or go on crying. If you have a choice (and you do) you might just as well go on laughing. It's more joyful.

Spirit is joyful, and the nature of the Soul is joyful. The personality isn't always joyful, but it is part of the illusions of the physical level. The personality may feel lost, but there are no lost Souls. The Soul always knows where it is. It just doesn't care. It *knows* it's going to outlast the body, mind, and emotions, so why shouldn't it be happy in these lower worlds? And because the Soul has little concern about time or space, it is unconcerned with the trials of the physical, emotional, or mental levels. It moves into the physical body, inhabits it, and has a wonderful time doing the divine dance of God. In the midst of your personality trivialities, the Soul is laughing. So go ahead and just be happy.

If It'll Be Funny Later, It's Funny Now

When you can look at your life in perspective, you will see the humor of it. Enjoy it. Enjoy yourself in all your escapades. When you do, it's easy for the loving to come present and manifest itself in everything you do, and laughter is love being demonstrated and expressed. It's so good and healing to be able to laugh at yourself and with yourself. If you take yourself too seriously, you are probably going to fall to your knees before too long and have the world on your back. That may be a very hard burden.

The ultimate is what we're dealing with. Along the way towards the ultimate, you can have a lot of people, a lot of things, a lot of experiences, a lot of laughs, a lot of jokes, a lot of illnesses, a lot of happiness. The Bible talks about how there's a season for this and a season for that, and you just participate in what season you care to and allow other people to participate the same way. In that you'll find your freedom. In the Spirit you'll find your liberation.

And if that's all going to happen, we might just as well laugh and live in grace.

If It's Not Fun, Why Do It?

If you stay focused in the now, you can have tremendous joy and great fun wherever you find yourself. It's all your attitude, and your attitude is your choice. So if you're down, do whatever is necessary to change depression and discouragement to the positive energy of fun and laughter. Go to a funny movie. Go out with some friends and have a good time. Tell yourself jokes. Tickle yourself. Sing. Chant. Start laughing.

In MSIA we do have a lot of fun. If someone wants to join us, that's fine. If they don't, that's fine, too. We just continue having a great time, and if I'm not having fun, you probably won't find me doing it.

Gratitude Is a Powerful Antidote to Negativity

When you are in a state of heartfelt gratitude for your life and everything in it, you have discovered a spiritual truth.

One of the most beautiful and gratifying of all prayers is just saying, "Thanks." In reality, that is the only prayer necessary. If you surrender to God's will and something seemingly negative happens, just say, "Thank you, Lord," and look for the growth within it. You can also be grateful that God is involved—directly involved—in your life. Be grateful that He is purifying whatever needs to be purified, making sure that you learn the lessons you're here to learn, and taking you higher and higher all the time. Ultimately, you can't do anything "wrong," because God is with you, in you as you, and is making sure that it all comes out perfectly. And that is a lot to be thankful for.

An attitude of gratitude is also a key to being in harmony with infinite supply. When you can honestly and truly thank God for what you have, for all your experiences, for all the people in your life, and for all your expressions, the sense of gratitude goes very deep. In that depth, you are open to infinite supply.

You also might think about being grateful when your desires are *not* being fulfilled. You might think about being grateful when your prayers are *not* being answered. Let those desires and prayers go, and ask only for the highest good, that you might be free of the creation of desire, that you might be free from illusion, that you might be free to know your own Soul and its perfection and glory.

Sometimes the best way to make the most out of a situation is to get out of it. The other way is to accept it and be grateful that it isn't worse. I find that it's much easier to just love it all. When it shows up, I go, "Wow. Another form of loving. Another face of loving. Another expression of loving. Another location of loving." And then I get to participate in it. That's grateful.

As you accept what you have and give thanks for your blessings, you find your life becoming happier and happier. Because, truly, my friends, you are blessed. There is not one of you who is not continually receiving of God's infinite blessings and grace.

The Physical Level Is the Classroom

This physical level is the most insecure, the most doubt-ridden, and the most frustrating level, but that's because it is the classroom. The earth is one of those places where the Soul can get the most experience in the shortest period of time, so it chooses to come here as often as is necessary for the correct and useful experiences and to clean up incompletes from past existences. The Soul needs these experiences so it will know how to be an effective and efficient creator.

Our life reveals to us what we have to learn next—not to reveal our failure to us, but to reveal to us where we lacked preparation, where we really weren't thoroughly up on what was going on. So realize that there are valuable lessons to be learned from and in the "games" of the world—and if you were not still in the process of learning and growing, you would no longer be here in a physical body.

Live from the Inside Out

Truly, the last frontier is inside of you. When you can enter your loving, your spiritual center, it doesn't much matter what the world presents to you. You have the inner resources to create your own happiness and fulfillment. It is when you rely on something or someone else to make you happy and to bring you fulfillment that you can fall flat on your face. That is when you may have given up your responsibility to yourself.

Jesus told us, "But seek ye first the kingdom of God, . . . and all these things shall be added to you" (Matthew 6:33). Through misinterpretation of that statement, man has often worshiped an outer God, looking for God somewhere in a church building, a temple, a tabernacle, on the top of a mountain, on the bottom of the ocean, on the moon, etc. We did not hear the rest of the directive, which is that "the kingdom of God is within you" (Luke 17:21). You can't be much more specific than that.

In this world, it is important to carefully select the actions and expressions with which you involve yourself. It is often wise to say, "I'm not doing that. I don't want to be a part of that. I am not against you or the thing you are doing, but for my own balance I must declare that I don't want to be involved with that action." You do have a right to declare your own balance. In fact, it is your divine responsibility to declare it.

You don't need to search outside yourself for direction. You can simply move into your own wisdom anytime you choose and live your life from that reality. So always remain true to that clear center within you that tells you your direction. Listen within to the message of Spirit, your own Spirit, your own consciousness of the Beloved. All wisdom is available to you at every moment. It is your challenge and your responsibility to attune yourself to Spirit and to the God within so that you may receive the wisdom from yourself. And if you can see beyond the words written on this page, if you see and recognize the truth in the ideas expressed here, it is only because the truth in you knows the truth out here. That part of you that knows the truth, knows what is being taught.

All love is within you. If you enter your inner world in love and if you maintain that love, you can live more freely and effortlessly. The loving heart shoots up like a fountain, into all of life. Whoever encounters a loving nature can be lifted, and as you express your loving, everyone around you can be touched and awakened.

So realize that your world is inside of you. Radiate your inner Light. Build it and let it shine. Spirit lives in the inner consciousness. Its voice rings in the silence of your spiritual heart. Its movement is in the perfect stillness within. Its greatest expression is in the peace and loving that reside at the core of your beingness. So don't look for God and Spirit outside yourself. Just awaken to the presence inside, and know that God reigns personally inside you as you and that the Beloved is present.

You Are a Creator

If I could really get you to understand that you are the source *individually* of all things around you, you would have the knowledge necessary for your life to come abundantly to you. For you are a creator, a divine creator, if you will. You are placed on the planet with everything you need already inside you. You can't be upset unless you allow it. You can't be controlled unless you allow it. This puts you in a unique position. And since you are a creator, you can create discord or harmony, despair or happiness, depression or joy, productiveness or apathy.

Spirit is the unseen, the invisible. Spirit is neutral and allows us to shape It within ourselves. If you shape Spirit negatively, then that is what you get. If you shape It positively, *that* is what you get, and if you're wise, you'll also shape It lovingly. So use your wisdom to make the choices that support you, and live a life of preferences, denying nothing, making choices in a positive direction.

God's power is inherent in your being through the Soul. It is the pearl of such great price that to reach it, you must undergo a transformation of consciousness and learn to take full responsibility for what you put in motion. You learn to complete what you begin. If your creation is of the physical world, complete it here. If it is of the imagination, finish it there. If it's emotional, resolve it in the emotions. If it is of the mind, finish your thoughts. Don't start things you don't intend to finish. Watch carefully your commitments in the world. Keep them realistic, and only make commitments you can keep. When you do, you can experience greater freedom.

When negativity is present, you do not have to participate in it. You have a choice. You are in control. You are the one deciding what to do in your life. And you have to be very careful of the thoughts you allow to dwell in your mind. Keep them positive and uplifting so that you send a positive form out into the formlessness of Spirit. If you're going to think, think wonderful, beautiful, uplifting things. Let the mind be a tool for your upliftment.

And the spiritual heart always knows the truth. Whenever you wonder how the spiritual heart can lead you, start by asking yourself, "Is this the right action for me?" If the heart sings a song of love, go. If there is no response or there is doubt, steer clear. This is your guide. This is love leading you.

Moving your inner awareness into your Soul is easy, but it's just as easy to lose that awareness. You can fall out of awareness because the world doesn't seem to support spiritual awakening. Spirit lets you in easily, but It has to give way to the materiality of the world. The material world has a billion distractions, so it's necessary to watch where you place your focus and your motivation for creating what you want. If you want to know God, keep your eyes on God.

So get your priorities straight, and place only God in front of you. Everything else is going to corrupt, decay, and fall apart. Know where your real value is, and choose where you place your energies and what is important to you. Sacrifice everything in this world for your knowledge of God. Each day, you need to choose the experience of your Soul. It is always your decision.

Sick and Tired of Being Tired and Sick

You cannot have what you want where you are, or you would already have it. This is spiritual law. You must move from where you are to get what you want. And sometimes you will make changes in your life when you simply get sick and tired of being tired and sick. You may have to disturb yourself in order to become aware of yourself, in order to establish a reference point for your progress and to know that you are forever moving upward in your spiritual progression, moving always into the heart of God.

Your agony, your melancholy, and your despair result from slowly trying to reveal yourself to yourself, to accept your own God consciousness and your own Christ Light within. That is what all the suffering is. And you sometimes fight "tooth and toenail" to hang on to the old things you have always used, even though they are not working for you.

When you are working with the Traveler, it will move

into your consciousness, through love, and start loving the pain out of you. The Traveler can place more love within you than you can create pain. That's one of the things that makes working with the Traveler very nice. Can the pain really be dissolved? Sure, it can just be wiped away. It happens all the time during aura balances. It happens during seminars, as you read the Soul Awareness Discourses, and when you do your spiritual exercises. But it also happens in perfect timing, as you can use it and handle it, for your highest good. The pain releases as you learn to let it go, as you have the wisdom and the courage to say, "I can't take the hurt. I can't take the pain. I'm going to do everything I can not to take pain, not to give pain, not to promote pain, and not to be involved in pain." That's good. That's smart. That's paradise. That's heaven.

Win in Your Fantasy

Don't lose in your fantasy. Always win in your fantasy because you're making it up. Don't make it up as bad; make it up as good.

When you worry, you're holding pictures in your mind that you want *less* of, but the law of Spirit says, "What you focus upon, you become. What you focus on comes to you." So hold in your mind what you want *more* of.

God Is Your Partner

If you are an initiate of the Traveler, progressing through the various levels of initiation, you become more and more powerful as you become more and more closely attuned to the Light and the Sound and the source within you that is God. Your very thoughts become prayers, and if those thoughts are energized through your emotions, you can create extremely quickly and effectively that which you desire. So it makes a good deal of sense to monitor your desires and, if you find them aligned with your deepest goals, to work with God as your partner.

In MSIA, that is done primarily through tithing and seeding. Tithing is about placing God first in your life, and being a joyful giver is a great part of loving the Lord with your body, mind, and Soul. For our time, tithing goes back to the time of Abraham, when he gave to the high priest, Melchizedek. But when Jesus incarnated, the old law of tithing was superseded by a new process under the Christ.

So we take the old law and move it around to realign it with the new energy flow. When you tithe to MSIA, you tithe in that new energy flow under the Christ. That means when you tithe out of your goodness and gratitude, there is going to be a lot of grace coming your way. And people who tithe in MSIA experience incredible things. They don't necessarily experience money things, but they experience a freedom of the Spirit in them. It's like it's no longer in bondage.

God said, "Ten percent of everything you own comes to Me first. Any increase you get, I get 10 percent first. That's Mine." What He really should have said is, "It's all Mine, and you can have 90 percent." Tithing is a way of saying, "God, pour forth whatever blessing You have for me." It's very true that if you tithe, you know God, but it is also true that if you want to know God, you tithe. The statement works both ways.

Seeding is a spiritual action because God is your partner. In a way, tithing is saying, in essence, "God, thank you for what I have received." Seeding is for future effect and is done beforehand. It works in the same sense as when you pray over your food and say, "Thank you, God, for what I am about to receive." Seeding has to have a value from inside of you placed upon what you are seeding for. And also try to have a picture of it so that there's an object for Spirit to move into.

Grace comes to you from God, through seeding, in so many ways—most of which you won't even be consciously aware of. For example, your seed may prevent negative things from coming in to you that you don't know about, which then allows the things that you want to come forward. God always supplies my seeding—always—not necessarily the way I wanted it, because it may not be good for me to have what I have seeded for. Sometimes it's not what you get that's the blessing; it's what you don't get.

You tithe and seed to the source of your spiritual teachings, and for those studying with the Mystical Traveler, that is MSIA. But you need to remember that *God* is your partner here—not me, not the Church. You're doing this between you and God.

Tithing and seeding, done with the right attitude of giving, can open your spirit and bring you to an inner peace by balancing some of the karmic blocks that have stood in your way. And if, on top of that, you get the material things, you're getting your cake and eating it, too.

Is God your partner? If the answer is yes, then you don't have any problems. And it's very hard for people to shake you loose from your spirit if you've done both tithing and seeding.

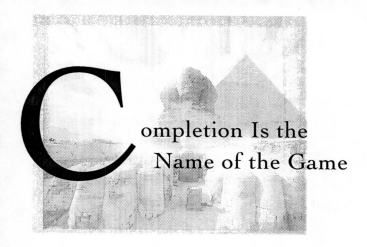

Completion Is the Name of the Game

This life is very easy. Do and complete, do and complete, do and complete, do and complete—no karma. Say you're going to do and then not do—karma. Start to do and then not finish—more karma. Feel bad about all that—more karma. It's obvious we've got more karmas than we've got completions.

Some incompletions apply to things you have around you. So simplify your life. You don't need all the clutter you are holding on to. Get rid of it now because it is stealing your energy; clutter actually takes energy to maintain. Start with the smallest things. If you clear away a little, you'll be amazed at the vast amounts of energy it can release inside of you. Keep around you only the things that give you energy.

And many times what you are involved in is wrapped up in memories that keep dragging you back to the past. Completion does not necessarily mean being finished physically. You can declare something completed by just saying, "It's done. I'm not going to do it anymore. It's finished just as it is."

In all of this, the challenge is to make your mind hold a focus until you complete the action of your thought. If you learn only that, you will have overcome this earth.

Spirit Is Always *Now*

Now is the only moment. This is it. This is all there is, so enjoy it. You can still have aspirations and plans and visions; just place them where you can realistically handle them, and that starts with right here and now.

To accomplish living in the now, you hold the emotions in an "up" consciousness, keep the mind focused on completion in the present moment, and keep the body healthy and able to hold the energy of Spirit. When you can do this, the consciousness expands to greater capabilities. Then comes the responsibility of holding your energies more in that greater field, and, of course, your reward is the ability to do more. Then your consciousness can expand to an even greater capability.

So don't worry about the future. When you're not living in expectation, you're less likely to be caught in negativity. Don't live in the imagination of what might happen. Instead, visualize the presence of God so you can have that. Then if you walk into any negativity, you walk right on through.

And don't worry about the past. You cannot live yesterday. Memory isn't what the heart desires. The heart desires fulfillment now, on this level, in this moment. So don't be concerned about yourself. All things are already being taken care of. The true self is moving you forward on your divine destiny, and you do not have to look at your past actions. And if you begin with what's true for you in this moment and work with that and don't focus on negative things in the past that have "gone wrong," you may find that things will begin clearing.

The mind changes, the emotions betray, the body falls apart, the personality alters, but the living heart of the Christ lives on eternally. Eternity is now. The eternal now is always present, and each moment, each breath, is a divine gift. Each breath is an opportunity to remember and worship God.

Man Is to Have Joy and Have It More Abundantly

When God awakened and moved upon Himself and breathed forward all the worlds, He did it for Himself, which is within each Soul. He did it for each one of us to come into this experience and have happiness and joy beyond all imagining.

The literature of Spirit says you are to have joy and have it more abundantly. It does not say that you are to have fulfillment through sensuous activities. It says *joy,* and joy is inherent through the Soul. When you have joy—when this happiness just comes up inside of you—then no matter what you do or say or become out there, this center of calm and happiness is not disturbed because it is what it is. Therein is your fulfillment for being on this level.

And when something makes you joyfully happy, even though you can't see, touch, feel, hear, or smell it, you're tapping into Spirit. When you feel the joy and goodness bubbling up inside of you for no apparent reason, you're in Spirit. When you feel like laughing and nothing is particularly funny, but the laughter is just an overflow of the good feeling inside, you are in Spirit. It's the peace that goes beyond understanding and the love that stays present no matter what other people do.

Although the very nature of the Soul, which you are, is happiness and joy, that which is the true self has been beguiled, and it searches out in the illusions of the world to find happiness. It is not there, for happiness is within. Happiness is the Soul. Even in the midst of aches and pains, emotional anguish, and negative thinking, there can be joy and love because those are of the Soul. And to participate consciously in Soul awareness, you must come into harmony with its joyful nature. So cultivate joyfulness in yourself and everything you do. Joyfulness is more real than your problems. When you are focused on God, joy is always present, even in the midst of your fear, apprehension, anxiety, expectation, doubt, sorrow, and concern.

You can be joyful on the physical level. If you're going to scrub the floor, do it as a dance. The Soul can be dancing through the mop, the brush, and the water, and scrubbing the floor can become a joyful expression of Spirit. You can approach anything and everything you do with Spirit—100 percent.

You can be joyful in the emotions. The positive level of the emotions is a joyful, blissful feeling. It's a good feeling towards all of God in all Its manifest forms throughout all creation, and it's the action of truly exemplifying the loving heart. Long ago, I told myself that whenever a feeling of depression came over me, it would immediately move me to joy. In other words, I reprogrammed depression for happiness. Anything less than a state of loving can be used to reprogram you back into a state of loving. Anything off-center can be used to move you back to center.

You can be joyful in the mind. The mind can never comprehend Spirit, but the heart *knows* Spirit. And when you can shut up your blabber mind long enough to listen to the spiritual heart, you can find yourself in living love—in the eternal presence of God—and that becomes a joyful occasion.

You can bring more joy into your life, and it's difficult to have a whole lot of joy when you have a lot of karma keeping your nose to the grindstone. You have to be able to look up once in a while and see the essence of Light pouring down on you. This is one of the values of MSIA seminars, Soul Awareness Discourses, and getting together with people who are also living the Light. It gives you a vision and the strength of the group. And it gives you a concentrated dose of the Holy Spirit that can come through when people are gathered together in the Light.

So let's live in the Spirit of Light, love, happiness, and joy, and let's find God within and God without. And as you awaken more to the Spirit within you, you will see it more in others. You will begin to see Spirit everywhere. You will see everything as a part of God, and everything you see will lift you because it will continuously direct you to God. What a joyful day that is!

Dishonesty Forfeits Divine Aid

If you approach things in a dishonest way from any level, you are on your own, you have forfeited divine aid, and you will get to handle the consequences on your own terms. So let's look at *where* the divine aid is actually forfeited. We say that the Kingdom of Heaven is within. So if dishonesty forfeits divine aid, where must you be dishonest in order to forfeit divine aid? Inside of yourself.

In terms of a business, for example, if you and the people working with you run your business in honesty and in loving service—not only in your dealings with each other but also in your dealings out there in the world—it is really easy for Spirit to put Its energy there. But if deception, deceit, dishonesty, etc., enter into the business on any level, then Spirit is automatically blocked from entering in on any level.

And say you have found yourself not doing what you profess. When you are honest and say, "Yes, I have been hypocritical on many things," you are open to receive of the essence of spiritual energy. But if you deny what is so, you can shut yourself down, and Spirit cannot come into a closed place. So if you deny something that is going on internally, the condition you are in or how you got there, it's very difficult to do anything to change, improve, or correct it.

Integrity Is Having the Courage to Go with the Truth as You Know It, as a Heartfelt Response, with Care and Consideration for Others

Integrity is an indicator, in the physical world, of spirituality. No one can force you to live up to the best within yourself; no one can make you obey your conscience. Imagine doing those things because you choose to. That's integrity.

When you come into that place of integrity, everything you do is done with a sense of completeness, honesty, nowness, and trueness. But first and foremost, you have to realize it inside yourself. So do yourself a favor. Live honestly, with integrity, with loving kindness and charity for your fellow beings. Your reward will be your ability to do better and the awakening of Spirit inside of you to higher levels of expression.

And be totally honest with yourself. Don't con yourself into thinking things are what they are not. You don't have to defend anything. When you drop the defenses and just acknowledge what is, you may find that you suddenly perceive much more clearly what you're doing. As soon as you move to that which is going on and forget the wishful thinking or the hopeful layout of what you want to take place, the further you will be along the path of reality. So live your life the way it *is,* not the way you'd like it to be, the way you think it ought to be, or the way your parents told you it should be. Live your life as it is.

When you simply let your own self, which is God, shine through, there is such freedom because you never have to pretend to be something you're not. If you're feeling particularly loving and positive, that's fine. If you're not, that's fine, too. It's okay to be whoever you are in the moment. Just be who you are and let that be enough—because it is. When you recognize what is and work with it, you can find that your honesty is your power, your security, and your key to the next level of progression.

So don't try to hide your mistakes and errors in consciousness. You cannot hide them from your Soul; it is your own Soul to which you are held accountable. If you've made an error, own it, and take the steps necessary to correct it. There is no disgrace in that. There is an integrity that brings with it a tremendous freedom.

With freedom comes responsibility to yourself, that inner integrity. When freedom comes before integrity, you can get yourself in trouble. When integrity walks hand in hand with freedom, it's a combination that can lift you very high in Spirit. With integrity and freedom, your inner life and outer life match; there is one reality in your life, and it's easy to live from that reality. You merge the outer life with the inner life and live from a spiritual form through the physical form in the world.

And in your relationships with others, be honest. If someone you are close with does something that annoys you, tell them. Don't let it go on and on, with irritation building inside until it starts manifesting in all sorts of strange and unrelated ways. Tell them. Give your loved ones a chance to participate with you. And if your spouse, a loved one, or a friend has the courage to be honest with you, let them know you appreciate it and give them loving support so they have the freedom to be more of who they are with you. It will be tremendously rewarding for both of you.

Honesty can be a great expression of loving. When you share with a person in *loving* honesty, you do not hurt or push away the person. You assist the person to a new level inside himself or herself. And remember that "being honest" is not license to jam your opinion at someone or to hurt them in the name of "truth." Always be loving in your approach.

When you are honest with yourself and with others, you truly can "die" to this world each night as you go to sleep and be free in your consciousness to travel the inner worlds to God. If you have situations pulling on you from the day, then you may hold yourself in the body and not get free. The Traveler may not be able to take you into Soul because your mind and emotions are still fighting to resolve the turmoils of the day. Do yourself a favor and be honest in your daily life, and then you can lay it down and travel freely in the night travel. And you'll find that you can live more freely during the daytime, too.

So walk always in the truthfulness of your spiritual heart. When you are living from the truth of your own beingness, you can become very realistic about what is and can perceive and work with what is—without having to make any value judgments in your mind and emotions. That will be a great freedom to you. You will become able to perceive more and more clearly and with less and less judgment. You will see things for what they are and work from that level. It's a good place to be. That's the way to find God.

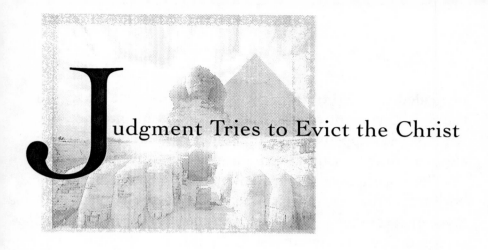

Judgment Tries to Evict the Christ

There is no way under the sun that you can rise to God consciousness and maintain any form of contempt. It will block you. Having contempt for God is having contempt for all things, and if you have contempt for your father or your daughter or a boss or a table or a race of people or a hair style or yourself, then you have contempt for the great God that is in all things. As soon as you judge, you strike against divine love. And when you judge yourself, feel bad about yourself, and think that you are not worthy or worthwhile, you are choosing the negative. You deny the grace of the Christ, which is available to you at all times.

You do not have to judge your experiences; all you have to do is complete them. You're not expected to know what is happening all the time or to make sense out of what is happening around you. And as soon as you measure your present experience with a past experience, you have judged it, and your judgments will be upon you. You have then propelled yourself out of Spirit. To get yourself back into the Spirit, you move into the present moment and love whatever is happening, because when you are not living in expectation, you can't be caught in negativity.

The spiritual energy will flow naturally to the areas within you that are most "asleep." It will move to the next layer or level that needs to be awakened and brought into a greater level of awareness. Be patient with yourself in that process. Allow Spirit to do Its work without hampering It by making judgments and beating yourself up. And if the Light illuminates your faults, let go of your feeling that you have to overcome them. You only have to get beyond them, to let them go, to repent, which means that you do not repeat your error.

We will all have a chance to look back at how we have lived. If you have lived your life and place no blame anywhere—for your "success" or for your "failure"—then when that time comes to look, you'll find that you will be very merciful to yourself.

You can also be merciful to others. Regardless of behavior, appearance, or presentation, every human being is involved in their own particular rate of spiritual progress. Their own rate is their divine right. It's of much greater value to love them than to judge or criticize them.

Letting the love flow through can be very easy. All you do is move to a neutral position—not one of belief or disbelief, not one of judgment or prejudice, but one of receptiveness. As soon as you judge, you strike against love, so take the attitude that no matter where you look, no matter what you see, it is a manifestation of love. That which you see is love in front of you. Love may be many different sizes, shapes, and forms, but it is all love. And how do you get out of the cycle of negative judgment? Consecrate your life to God, to Spirit, and do everything in God's name.

Forgiveness Is the Key to the Kingdom

Sometimes you may still fall into the trap of thinking that if you're really spiritual and really living the Traveler's teachings, nothing will ever upset you, you won't make any mistakes, and you'll be able to smoothly handle anything that comes your way. And it just doesn't seem to happen that way. Sure, you might get upset sometimes. Sure, you might get hurt sometimes. But you don't have to hold on to it forever and ever. You can own up to it, let it go, and move on.

In Soul, you step free from the past. There is nothing you have done that you cannot transcend because you are greater than any of your actions. So whatever has happened in the past, with whomever, over whatever, is past. It is as simple as that because it's *past*. And whether they were right or wrong, whether you did or you didn't do it, whether they did or they didn't—all that is immaterial. Don't waste your time on it. And if you had a difficult

171

childhood and your parents did some things that weren't the best, you can let that go, take responsibility for where you are right now in your life, and change anything that you are still holding on to from childhood.

There is no vacuum in these universes. The Spirit is everywhere. So when you relax a position and let it go, the Spirit, the Light, will fill that space. And when you are attuned to Spirit and are experiencing the love of Spirit, the negativity of others does not matter, and your own negativity does not matter. There is love and forgiveness for everything and everyone.

So sacrifice any negative images of yourself and realize that whatever your transgressions, you are a spiritual being worthy of God's love and Light. In this, you forgive yourself and lift once again into the more positive expression. You can do this instantly; you do not have to prolong the punishment of separation and denial. For there is nothing that is not forgiven. There is no Soul that is ever abandoned or lost. So keep forgiveness and unconditional love flowing, for yourself and all others.

If we're going to live a life of health, wealth, and happiness and prosperity and loving and caring and sharing, then we're going to have to just forgive everything as the Christ forgives and go on living the life of enlightenment. What a challenge, but it is so easy.

Peace Is the Cessation of Againstness

Peace, according to my concept, is the natural state of humankind. We are the children of a benevolent Creator, and peace is our eternal home. Peace is God, Spirit, the One—whatever word you want to call it—and peace is always available.

When you're not against anything or anyone, you start to feel the presence of peace. And being for yourself does not mean being against anyone else. Since we are all one, being for yourself is ultimately only being for everyone else in your life. When you awaken to that truth and begin to live it, life will start opening for you, and joy will flood into you.

Although peace is the absence of againstness, internally and externally, it's not the absence of sandpapering, refining, and moving towards excellence. There can be divergent points of view without having "war." I call it conversation, communication, dialogue, and sharing ideas. It's integrity, which allows all people their moment to speak their truth.

Don't plan on there being no conflict in your life. Conflict can exist within peace, but you don't have to have againstness about it. You can say, "I disagree with that and that whole approach. I was there, and I didn't see that." That's a form of conflict, but it's not againstness. Againstness is more like, "You stupid idiot, I was there. I know what was going on. Wake up!" That's againstness, and you don't get to the road of peace and love and joy by traveling the path of lust and anger and revenge.

So whenever you hear of any negativity, instead of adding to it by condemning the people involved, send Light and love to everyone, even to those who have "messed up." Start adding peace to the situation through your compassion, acceptance, and understanding. And as you bring yourself into a loving consciousness with all things and with the One consciousness that is everywhere, peace and harmony will enfold your heart and you will recognize within every level of your beingness that there is only love.

Service Is the Highest Form of Consciousness on the Planet

Taking care of yourself is a way of serving yourself. And if you want to experience the Christ in your everyday life, the answer is very simple: serve, serve, serve. I should say, serving, serving, serving. Serving means getting up and going and doing what's in front of you to do. I think we find the Christ more readily in that serving than we do in anything else. In the Bible, Christ says, "All men will know that you are my disciples if you love one another" (John 13:35). How do we know that you do love one another? You help each other, you work with each other, and you support each other. And you just don't judge each other.

It may be necessary to let others experience their pain and tension so that they can understand what these things are and be prepared for greater things that may be coming later. They have to learn how to handle difficulties and discover their own solutions to their difficulties. Everyone grows by this process. To take things from people is to deny

175

them their own God consciousness. Don't worry. They'll find the solutions. They'll discover their own paths. If you point the way to the Light, they'll find their own ways. There is an old saying: "Give a man a fish, feed him for a day; teach a man to fish, feed him for a lifetime." If you teach people to fish, they will feed themselves. They're free and you're free. In freedom, the loving can be perfect. So discover where you can assist, rather than interfere. Assistance is a very beautiful form of loving.

I get letters from people who say, "You've taught me so much and I've taken from you for so long. How can I start giving back?" You can manifest the Spirit more completely in your life and give that Spirit to others. Give love. Give understanding. Don't preach to people. Just live with them in the fullness of your love. Become God's faithful servant, experiencing the joy that comes with serving unconditionally.

Love Is the Savior of Us All

Love is all-powerful. Jesus the Christ manifested living love by entering into this dimension and taking on everything, for all present and for all time. Jesus the Christ, the manifest reality, stood forward and said, "I come for all"—and that includes everyone, every single person, no matter what their expression.

Living love is loving yourself first, so that you can love others. It's taking care of yourself, so you can help take care of others. It's doing those things that are good for you, so that you'll be happy, healthy, and a joy to be with. So learn to be unconditionally loving towards yourself. Your relationship with yourself is more important than all the others, except your "relationship" with God. In reality, your relationship with God and your relationship with yourself are one and the same. And when love comes to you, don't refuse it by thinking you are not worthy. You are worthy, or love couldn't come your way.

There is little you can do in any situation with an individual that will do anything for them, short of loving them completely. So give love. Don't tell people what to do. Instead, just support them with your love. That's the best gift of all. And when you experience the loving within you and allow others in so they can experience your loving, you can find your own love growing.

Above all, what is important for you is to keep calling forward the essence of spiritual love every day so you keep lifting higher. Let nothing stop you from this endeavor. It is more important than any other activity. Love awakens us. When you experience the unlocking and unfolding of your spiritual heart, your loving nature, thank God from your deepest being that this is happening to you.

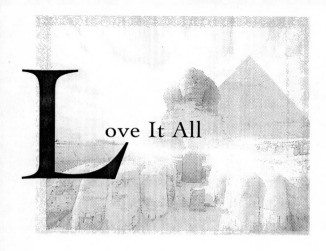

Love It All

Loving is the most important quality you can nurture in yourself. Your love needs to extend unconditionally to *all* things. You love everything present, no exceptions. Love it all, own it all, and then you will be free.

Even when you don't feel like loving, you love the feeling of not feeling like loving. And you treat your loving and your depression as equal. Anxiety, love, depression, happiness—they must all be treated equally. When you do, there can be no place for anything "better" or "worse" inside of you, so judgment ceases to have power in your consciousness. When you treat your depression the same as your loving, then neither has more power than the other, and you are free to choose the expression you want.

And love your karma. It is your opportunity to learn. It is your opportunity to gain wisdom, and by loving even your negative creations, you can shift their energy and release karma. In fact, you have the opportunity to change the karmic flow of your life through your ability to be loving. By loving the God in yourself and others, you can move into a path of greater unfoldment. So instead of looking at the factors of your life and saying, "That's my karma, so I can't help it," you might say, "That's my karma, and I will fulfill it so I am free." You don't have to blame your life's difficulties on karma. Through loving, you can complete your karma.

As you learn to recognize the Soul, the divinity in each person, you will be able to love all you meet. And if you feel that someone messed up your life, you must love that one, also. That person is Spirit, too. That person is also a part of God, equal to yourself. You don't have to go sit at the person's feet; you can leave the person alone. But you must do it in neutral consciousness—neither positive nor negative.

And in the midst of all the apparent conflict and stupidity in this world, you can still love. You can still have compassion. You can still reach in and say, "I'll help anyway." That's Spirit and God manifesting through you to the God in all people. It is a gift for both you and them. It's what this world is all about.

Since the key is to be loving, you'll give up every consideration, every hesitation, and every reason not to be loving, and you'll be loving in every situation in your life. For enough love will handle all things. If you are having difficulty handling something, you don't have enough love for that thing. So your next step is laid out right in front of you: get some more love. Your job here is to experience. That's all you have to do. It is in the *loving* of your experience, the *loving* of your expression, that you discover the inner joy, the bliss that is your indication of the presence of the Traveler.

Baruch Bashan

Baruch bashan means "the blessings already are," and the frequency of these Hebrew words inherently conveys the blessings to your consciousness. All the blessings that will ever be present exist here and now, and all you do is move into the realization of those blessings.

Living in Grace

What is the work that you're here to do? The most immediate thing in front of you, and there are two choices: either live under the law of karma or live under God's grace of loving. You can have your choice. And the grace of God did not say for one minute that you won't have any pain. It just said you can live in the Spirit while you walk through this world.

So put your loyalty to the Soul and to your awareness of Soul—*right here and now.* Lift above the lower world and live in the grace that your own Spirit can bring to you. When you express loving towards one another, this holds you more in the consciousness of grace. In that consciousness of grace, all things are made new, and then each person resurrects to the consciousness of God and becomes the Beloved and walks with the consciousness of the Traveler right into the Heart of Hearts, right into God.

It Takes Great Courage to See the Face of God

One of the reasons it takes great courage to see the face of God is that you first have to see your own face clearly. You must look clearly and honestly at yourself and at all your creations. You must confront the negativity and dissolve the negativity you've placed out. It sometimes isn't easy.

The face of God lies on the other side of all the illusions of the physical, imaginative, emotional, mental, and unconscious worlds. The way to the other side is through all of that. With the grace of the Traveler, you can tap into the consciousness of the Soul and use that higher perspective to guide your way so that you do not get trapped once again in the highways and byways of the lower worlds.

To look at the face of God, you actually have to stand back and stop wanting; you have to let go of all desire patterns. What good does it do you to gain all of the physical world if you lose your awareness of the Soul?

You gain the strength to see the face of God by looking

187

at your own "dark side," by loving that which does not seem perfect, by continually choosing the positive flow of energy and infusing your consciousness with Spirit, and by changing those things which have been your stumbling blocks. And, still, your ability to see the face of God is based far more on your attitude than on what you do or don't do physically.

To see the face of God, you also have to see the face of God in all people. That does take a lot of courage because you have to continually move yourself past your personality, prejudices, and points of view, until you recognize your oneness with those other personalities out there. It also takes a brave person to see their own God-face and not fall into the conceit and the ego of that moment. It takes courage to say, "I am God, and I'm moving on into greater realization of that. I know that everyone else is also God, and we are all moving upward together."

So remember always that you are an heir to the throne. When you recognize this and step into spiritual consciousness, you are prepared to see God. You will see God, not in the physical body, but in the Soul body. It is only through Spirit that you can perceive Spirit. Just as you use your physical eyes to perceive the physical world, you must use your spiritual eyes to perceive those spiritual qualities.

The Price of Freedom Is Eternal Vigilance

Eternal vigilance is knowing that as long as you are in a physical body, you need to do those things that maintain your balance and uplift your Spirit. If you begin to let your discipline slide, the strength you have built can begin to go slack, and the subtle little thoughts against this person or that situation can begin to take their toll on your peace and happiness. There really is no rest on the spiritual path.

And it is in *this* moment that you must watch. It is in *this* moment that you must monitor your words, your actions, and your thoughts. And when you monitor everything you put into motion sexually, physically, emotionally, mentally, and financially, you start to create your freedom. So walk through your life and, at the same time, observe yourself so you can learn from your experiences. Stay conscious and aware. Freedom comes with awareness. If you go "unconscious" and allow yourself to be run by your emotions and your "stinking thinking," you may stay stuck in those levels.

So keep yourself balanced physically, emotionally, and mentally. Stay neutral and loving. Be honest in your approach to yourself and everyone around you. You might feel like you're "walking on eggshells" for these few years that you are here, but that's okay. You're not here for long, and the rewards are well worth the effort. And don't worry about five or ten or fifteen years of watching and learning, if this is your last incarnation. It will do you little good to rush through this life only to come back and rush through eighty more or to find out that you have 180 more to go because you weren't paying attention and were compounding your total existence rather than watching it this time.

And even when you're in the Soul, you still need to keep exercising awareness and eternal vigilance because the negativity here on this physical level tends to pull you back into the negative areas. You can be pulled back easily, simply through judging, blaming, separating, or in some other way shutting down your loving. So take care of yourself on all levels. Do not grow lazy in your approach to your own spiritual life. Do those things that will be uplifting. Be with other people who are following the upward path. Be loving to yourself and to others. Chant the sacred names of God. Watch yourself in every situation. With practice, that is the easiest thing in the world to do because it is easiest on you in the long run.

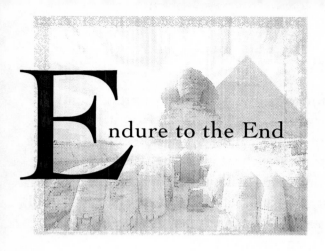

Endure to the End

Those of you who are climbing the inner path need only one blessing—endurance—for those who keep the spiritual law to the end and endure all things receive the most precious gift of Soul awareness, which is eternal life through eternal awareness on any level in any existence.

This means that no matter what happens, no matter how you feel, no matter how anybody else feels, no matter what you think, no matter what anyone else thinks, you go on. No matter what is or is not, you go on. You really have no other choice. So regardless of what is said, regardless of what happens, you always keep going on to the next thing. If you're right, you keep going. If you're wrong, you keep going. Right or wrong is not even a point of contention. Keep going. If you're in an illusion, go through it. If you're in truth, go on to greater truths.

And as you reach higher into Spirit, the things that were important to you in the first few years of your spiritual work are still important. It is still important to send the Light to people for the highest good. It is still important to ask for the Light to fill, surround, and protect you. It is still important to place the Light ahead of you in the activities of your day. It is still important to chant your initiation tone, for it is the foundation of your spiritual health. Don't let these habits slip from you as the years go by. They are your strength.

If you've been moving forward and upward in your spiritual progression and you get tired and decide you want to take a break, be careful. You won't be able to stand still. If you stop your forward progression, chances are you'll start slipping backwards. Those who have undergone adversity and maintained themselves in a positive focus of Spirit through all kinds of difficulties have gained the strength step-by-step to walk into the "high country." And if you have walked yourself up on the stepping-stones of your own experience, then even if you begin to slip backwards, you won't slide very far.

You reach into Spirit by building the strength of Spirit through spiritual exercises. You maintain your attunement with Spirit by continuing to do spiritual exercises, by listening to the Word of God spoken through your inner consciousness as well as in scripture and seminars, by chanting the name of God, and by riding the Sound Current back through the formlessness into the heart of God.

There Is Always "Et Cetera"

The teachings of the Movement are "et cetera," ETC, which means Eternally Traveling Consciousness. It has no period at the end because it goes on and on forever. You continue on in spite of everything. You disregard everybody and all situations that would block you. No matter what psychic influence impinges upon you, no matter who kicks you out the door, no matter how many times you get fired, no matter how many heart attacks you have—it's always et cetera. For your own movement of spiritual inner awareness is a progression, with no beginning and no end.

When you think you've reached the ultimate, look for what your next step will be. When you think you've learned all there is to learn, look for the one who will be your next teacher and awaken you to your next level. Remember that progression is infinite, so if you ever think you've got it made, recognize the et cetera coming up behind you. It's no big deal if you get caught in an illusion. You're going to get out of it because you're going on, so don't be concerned.

There can be no end to spiritual progression because there has never been a beginning. There is only a *now.* Even the Soul is not your ultimate goal. God is your ultimate goal. You do not stop when you reach Soul consciousness; you keep going, reaching into greater and deeper levels of God. And when you say, "This is it, I've found God," go on, because there is no limit in the spiritual realms. There is further and further progression, which is continuously becoming more aware. Each next step can take you further into your awareness of God and the joy of Spirit. So bless each step you take, and know that the Traveler walks with you.

Baruch Bashan

Glossary

astral realm. The psychic, material realm above the physical realm. The realm of the imagination. Intertwines with the physical as a vibratory rate.

aura. The electromagnetic energy field that surrounds the human body. Has color and movement.

baruch bashan (bay-roosh´ bay-shan´). Hebrew words meaning "the blessings already are."

Beloved. The Soul; the God within.

causal realm. The psychic, material realm above the astral realm and below the mental realm. Intertwines somewhat with the physical realm as a vibratory rate. The emotional realm. The start of cause and effect.

Christ Consciousness. A universal consciousness of pure Spirit. Exists within each person through the Soul.

Discourses. See Soul Awareness Discourses.

etheric realm. The psychic, material realm above the mental realm and below the Soul realm. Equated with the unconscious or subconscious level. Sometimes known as the esoteric realm.

high self. The self that functions as one's spiritual guardian, directing one towards those experiences that are for one's greatest spiritual progression. Has knowledge of the destiny pattern agreed upon before embodiment.

Holy Spirit. The positive energy of Light and Sound that comes from the Supreme God. The life force that sustains everything in all creation. Works only for the highest good. Is the third part of the Trinity or Godhead.

initiation. In MSIA, the process of being connected to the Sound Current of God.

initiation (initiatory) tone. In MSIA, spiritually charged words given to an initiate in a Sound Current initiation.

Inner Master. The inner expression of the Mystical Traveler, existing within a person's consciousness.

karma. The law of cause and effect: as you sow, so shall you reap. The responsibility of each person for his or her actions. The law that directs and sometimes dominates a being's physical existence.

Light. Living In God's Holy Thoughts. The energy of Spirit that pervades all realms of existence. Also refers to the Light of the Holy Spirit.

lower realms. See negative realms.

mental realm. The psychic, material realm above the causal realm and below the etheric realm. Relates to the universal mind.

Movement of Spiritual Inner Awareness (MSIA). A church whose major focus is to bring people into an awareness of Soul Transcendence. John-Roger is the founder.

mystery schools. Schools in Spirit, in which initiates receive training and instruction. Initiates of the Traveler Consciousness study in mystery schools that are under the Traveler's auspices.

Mystical Traveler Consciousness. An energy from the highest source of Light and Sound whose spiritual directive on Earth is awakening people to the awareness of the Soul. This consciousness has always been anchored on the planet through at least one person.

negative power. Functions out of the causal realm and sets up the karma of the planet. "The loyal forces of the opposition" that make sure people learn their lessons here.

negative realms. The realms below the Soul realm; namely, the physical, astral, causal, mental, and etheric realms. These are not "bad" but are like the negative pole of a battery. See also positive realms.

90-percent level. That part of a person's existence beyond the physical level; that is, one's existence on the astral, causal, mental, etheric, and Soul realms.

physical realm. The earth. The psychic, material realm in which a being lives with a physical body.

positive realms. The Soul realm and the 27 levels above the Soul realm. Like the positive pole of a battery. See also negative realms.

s.e.'s. See spiritual exercises.

seeding. A form of prayer to God for something that one wants to manifest in the world. It is done by placing a "seed" with (giving an amount of money to) the source of one's spiritual teachings.

seminar. A talk given by John-Roger or John Morton; also, an audiotape, CD, videotape, or DVD of a talk either of them has given.

Soul. The extension of God individualized within each human being. The basic element of human existence, forever connected to God. The indwelling Christ, the God within.

Soul Awareness Discourses. Booklets that students in MSIA read monthly as their spiritual study. An important part of the Traveler's teachings on the physical level.

Soul consciousness. A positive state of being. Once a person is established in Soul consciousness, he or she need no longer be bound or influenced by the lower levels of Light.

Soul realm. The realm above the etheric realm. The first of the positive realms and the true home of the Soul. The first level where the Soul is consciously aware of its true nature, its pure beingness, its oneness with God.

Soul Transcendence. The process of moving the consciousness into the Soul realm and beyond.

Sound Current. The audible energy that flows from God

through all realms. The spiritual energy on which a person returns to the heart of God.

Spirit. The essence of creation. Infinite and eternal.

spiritual exercises (s.e.'s). Chanting Hu, Ani-Hu, or one's initiation tone. An active technique of bypassing the mind and emotions by using a spiritual tone to connect to the Sound Current. Assists a person in breaking through the illusions of the lower levels and eventually moving into Soul consciousness. See also initiation (initiatory) tone.

10-percent level. The physical level of existence, as contrasted with the 90 percent of a person's existence that is beyond the physical realm. See also 90-percent level.

tithing. The spiritual practice of giving 10 percent of one's increase to God by giving it to the source of one's spiritual teachings.

Traveler. See Mystical Traveler Consciousness.

About the Author

For more than forty years, Dr. John-Roger's life has been devoted to the spiritual work of Soul Transcendence, the realization of oneself as a Soul and as one with the Divine. In the course of his work, he has traveled and spoken extensively throughout the world and written over fifty books, two of which have been on the *New York Times* Bestseller List. He has given over six thousand talks, and many are presented on his nationally seen television show, "That Which Is."

John-Roger is the founder and spiritual advisor of the nondenominational Church of the Movement of Spiritual Inner Awareness (MSIA); founder, first president, and now chancellor of the University of Santa Monica; founder and president of Peace Theological Seminary & College of Philosophy; founder and chairman of the board of Insight Seminars; founder and first president of the Institute for Individual and World Peace; and founder of the Heartfelt Foundation.

John-Roger's wisdom, humor, common sense, and love have helped people discover the Spirit within themselves and find greater health, prosperity, and peace, and he continues to transform lives by educating people in the wisdom of the spiritual heart.

For more information about John-Roger, you may also visit: www.john-roger.org

Soul Awareness Discourses
A Course in Soul Transcendence

Soul Awareness Discourses are designed to teach Soul Transcendence, which is becoming aware of yourself as a Soul and as one with God—not as a theory, but as a living reality. They are for people who want a consistent, time-proven approach to their spiritual unfoldment.

A set of Soul Awareness Discourses consists of 12 booklets, one to study and contemplate each month of the year. As you read each Discourse, you can activate an awareness of your Soul and deepen your relationship with God.

Spiritual in essence, Discourses are compatible with religious beliefs you might hold. In fact, most people find that Discourses support the experience of whatever path, philosophy, or religion (if any) they choose to follow. Simply put, Discourses are about eternal truths and the wisdom of the spiritual heart.

The first year of Discourses addresses topics ranging from creating success in the world to working hand in hand with Spirit.

A yearly set of Discourses is regularly $100. MSIA is offering the first year of Discourses at an introductory price of $50. Discourses come with a full, no-questions-asked, money-back guarantee. If at any time you decide this course of study is not right for you, simply return it, and you will promptly receive a full refund.

To order Soul Awareness Discourses, contact the Movement of Spiritual Inner Awareness at 1-800-899-2665 or order@msia.org, or visit the MSIA Store online at www.msia.org

Fulfilling Your Spiritual Promise

If you ever had a question for John-Roger,
chances are you'll find it answered here.

This 3-volume set of books by Dr. John-Roger is a compendium of information he has shared over many years. Along with an index that makes finding topics easy, its 24 chapters include a wealth of information on subjects including karma, the Mystical Traveler, initiation, and dreams, as well as attitude, relationships, health, and practical spirituality. And at just $45 for the whole set, this resource is a great buy. (ISBN: 978-1-893020-17-7. Hardbound, 3-book set, $45)

To order this book or other materials by John-Roger, contact the Movement of Spiritual Inner Awareness at 1-800-899-2665 or order@msia.org, or visit the MSIA Store online at www.msia.org

Printed in the United States
96195LV00001B/139-600/A